MAKING SILVER JEWELRY...

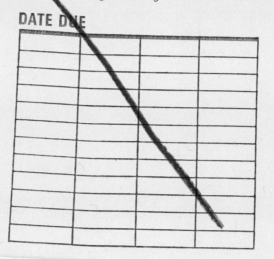

For Spunky, who will, hopefully,
want to use this some day in the future.

With thanks to Elaine Nippo, William Rydwels and Marga
Kassimir, who loaned some of their work for the photographs,
and to Phebe and Miss A., in hopes that they will forgive my
presumption.

MAKING SILVER JEWELRY

Nona Ziek

Illustrations by Marjorie Sablow
Photography by Marga Kassir

A BERKLEY WINDHOVER BOOK
published by
BERKLEY PUBLISHING CORPORATION

contents

introduction   11

CHAPTER ONE   13

*your materials
& how to use them*

CHAPTER TWO   23

getting started

CHAPTER THREE   29

*your tools
& how to use them*

APTER FOUR   53

bent wire
Hair ornament, Pendant, Finger ring,
Earrings

CHAPTER FIVE 65

unit construction
Earrings, Double-whorled bracelet,
Necklace

CHAPTER SIX 77

cages & wrappings
Pendant, Earrings with beads,
Ring with wrapped tumbled stone,
Wrapped shell pendant

CHAPTER SEVEN 87

stamped patterns
A textured open bracelet, Textured
spiral ring

CHAPTER EIGHT 95

sawed shapes
Earrings, Bracelet threaded on a
velvet ribbon

CHAPTER NINE 103

simple soldering
Ring, Double hoop earrings, Shoulder
bag hook

CHAPTER TEN 115

sweat-soldering
Belt buckle, Pendant with mixed metal
design, Cuff links

CHAPTER ELEVEN 127

twisted wire

Bangle made with two vises, Bangle
with round and half-round wires,
Square wire bangle, Flat wire bangle

CHAPTER TWELVE 137

tubing & beads

Earrings, Round tubing pendant

CHAPTER THIRTEEN 145

forging

Open bracelet, Hairpin, Earrings
with beads, Necklace

CHAPTER FOURTEEN 157

bezeled stones

Ring, Indian bolo slide, Cuff links
with square stones

CHAPTER FIFTEEN 169

pronged mounts

Pendant, A pin-pendant

IAPTER SIXTEEN 181

fusing

Belt buckle, A fused pin-pendant, Ring

CHAPTER SEVENTEEN   191

chains
Round wire chain, Beaded chain,
Motif chain

CHAPTER EIGHTEEN   203

granulations
&filigree
Hairpin, Pendant, Ring

CHAPTER NINETEEN   213

accidental shapes

REFERENCE LISTS
    Gem Stones   220
    Metal Gauges   224
    Solders   226
    Craft Organziations   227
    Sources & Suppliers   228
    Glossary   232
    Bibliography   237

MAKING SILVER JEWELRY

introduction

Ever since the Stone Age (and probably long before that) men and women have been making body ornaments. And so can you! Just as there's no trick to living like royalty on royal funds, there's no trick to owning magnificent jewels if you can afford a Cellini to make them for you. But however magnificent those jewels, they will represent only the jeweler's ideas. *You* can wear original jewelry, designed and made by the one person who best knows what you consider beautiful and suitable—yourself!

That's what this book is all about. It is dedicated to the proposition (to steal a phrase) that well-designed and individual pieces of jewelry can be made outside of a professional workshop on a minimum budget, with inexpensive and improvised tools, by anyone of any age (NOT 6-year-olds, please) and without previous design or art training. You will make jewelry worth hundreds of dollars, and each piece will be one-of-a-kind, well-made, original—in short, a creation!

You can work at a kitchen table, or spread out in a full workshop; you can work with a handful of simple tools, or splurge on a wealth of mechanical marvels; your designs can be carefully classic, or wildly off-beat in concept. However you choose to start this most fascinating of crafts, the end product will be personal, wearable, and valuable!

You will hear, again and again, the magic words, "You *made* that *yourself?* How wonderful!"

And it will be!

Plate 1: Silver goodies with ideas to stimulate your creativity.

your materials & how to use them

Silver is a wonderful material. It has both intrinsic monetary value and great natural beauty. It is the least expensive of the "precious" metals, and can be handled in so many ways that it offers endless possibilities for design. In its pure state, it is the whitest of metals, and no other metal has a more brilliant lustre. But in this state it is so plastic that it must be alloyed for strength and stability, so that a piece does not bend out of shape every time you put it on or remove it. Alloying means melting the pure silver with other metals. What you will use is an alloy called "Sterling," which has 925 parts of pure silver and 75 parts of copper.

All the metals used in commercial jewelry, from platinum and gold to copper, brass and even iron, have personal qualities. Not all these qualities are advantageous. Silver has more plus qualities and fewer minus qualities than any other metal. These plus-qualities include the fact that silver has great *malleability*. This means that it can be hammered

13

(forged) or rolled thin, without cracking. Silver is also very *ductile:* it can be drawn into very fine wire. It has *toughness,* so that it can be twisted and bent without breaking, and it can be worked in many ways. It responds to polishing better than any other metal, and it has the supreme advantage of being much less expensive than gold.

Silver used for jewelry making can be purchased in many forms: Sheet silver is bought according to gauge (thickness) by the square inch. The supplier may also sell according to weight as well as by dimension. Silver also comes in "wire" form: round, half-round, square, flat (or rectangular) and even triangular and oval (see Fig. 1). Here too, you must know what gauge you want to use before you order. Manufacturing jewelers, using special tools, "draw" their own wire, but the process is time-consuming and it pays to purchase small amounts ready-made. In this country, all silver is measured by the Browne & Sharpe gauge, with the gauge numbers increasing as the metal thins. So you will find that 8-gauge silver is much heavier than 20-gauge silver. Except for mounting stones, you will work mostly with 18-gauge, 16-gauge and 14-gauge metal.

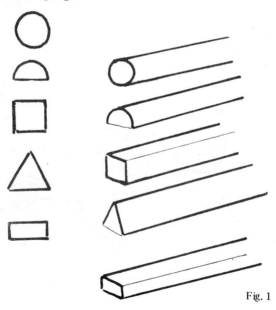

Fig. 1

Silver also can be bought as tubing: both round and square, and you will learn to use this too. While wire is usually ordered by the foot, tubing is often purchased by the inch. Since tubing comes in many diameters (see Fig. 2) you must know how you want to use it, and how much you want, as well as the size and shape.

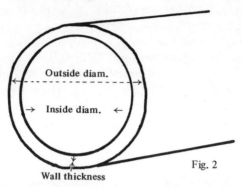

Fig. 2

All forms of metal working fall under one of two headings: the article is *shaped,* by any one (or more) of a number of methods, and the *surface* of the article is *decorated,* again using any one or combination of methods, some of which you are going to learn to do.

You can shape your piece of jewelry by *bending* it or by *twisting* it (see Fig. 3). As you will see with your first project, silver wire is easily bent by hand. When you have started to

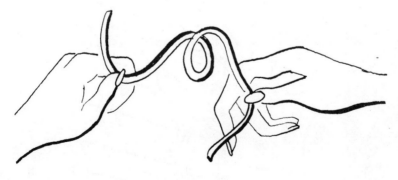

Fig. 3

Fig. 4

solder, pieces of different gauges of wire can be put together
(see Fig. 4). Silver wires, round, half-round, square or
rectangular, can be combined by twisting, to make lovely
bangles, open or closed (see Fig. 5). Bits of sheet silver can
also be twisted into shapes to make unusual designs and odd
settings for stones. Silver sheet can also be bent over various
forms to make curved patterns (see Fig. 6).

Fig. 5

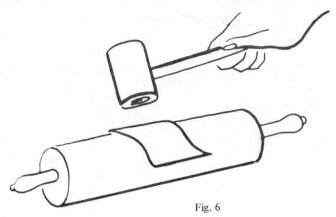

Fig. 6

One of the most common methods of shaping pieces of metal is called *cold forging* or the hammering of a metal over a form to create the shape. It is the technique by which the silversmith takes a flat disc of metal and turns it into a bowl or a pitcher. While you will not do this, you can, by means of forging, flatten part of a wire in a design, thin out your metal, and with light blows, harden the metal just enough to make it hold the shape you want. Without forging, your ring would lose shape with one wearing.

Even simpler is the process of *shaping with a saw*. The use of the jeweler's saw will give you two shapes at one time: a cut-out piece, and the frame from which the cut-out was sawed (see Fig. 7). Each can be used effectively, and in more

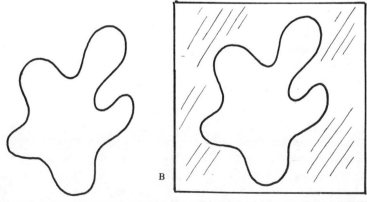

A   B

Fig. 7

than one way, and you will find that the part you rejected for one piece of jewelry, which finds its way into your scrapbox, will give you ideas for using it in a different way later on. The cut-outs can be soldered to solid pieces of sheet, or can be fused to sheet (or other bits or scrap) with direct heat. The outline-sections are also useful for soldering and fusing, and can be filled with enamels, niello or stones.

Finally, the silver can be shaped by *casting*. This means that the melted metal is poured into a mold to set. Molds have been prepared in sand, in cuttle-bone, or by the ancient method called "lost wax." Most casting is too complicated (and requires expensive equipment) for you to try. You can, however, try direct casting, using a crucible and a pot of cold water. You can get lovely "accidental" shapes by this method, but duplicating a desirable shape is usually difficult. Still, it is fun to try it, once you have mastered the more conventional methods.

Once the shape has been made, the surface can be *decorated*. When the design of the shape is important enough to stand alone (as with much of Scandinavian design) the surface decoration is simply polishing. The silver can also be antiqued, or darkened with liver of sulphate, and then polished on the high spots only, for definition and emphasis of the high-low aspects of the pattern. The surface can have lines filed into it, or it can be burned with a torch, so that it is roughened and blistered, and then polished. In part, or in whole, it can be gold-plated, like the beautiful medieval candlesticks and reliquaries, or it can be rhodium-plated for a brilliant high silver-gloss that never needs to be repolished.

All kinds of surface patterns can be made. *Granulations* (tiny balls of silver) and *filigree* (twists of very fine silver wire) can be applied (see Fig. 8). The design can be *chased*, with patterned punches hammered on the face of the metal (see Fig. 9). It can be *engraved*, with special tools that remove fine threads of metal and leave a sunk-in design. It can be *hammered* (see Fig. 10) with different hammers and different parts of the hammer faces, to make dents of various size and shape, on part of the piece or over the entire face. Other pieces of the silver (or of other metals) can be *soldered* on top to make a design, and layers of pattern can be made this way (see Figu. 11 und 12), or otherwise withnut the use of solder

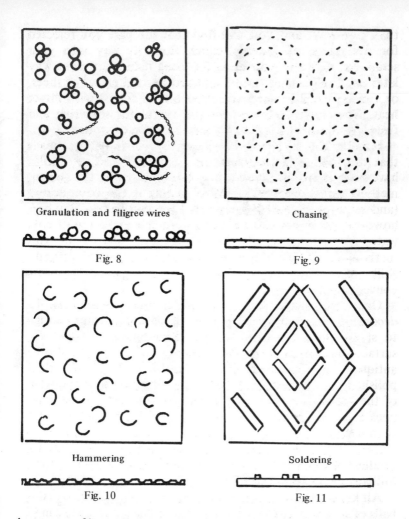

Granulation and filigree wires

Fig. 8

Chasing

Fig. 9

Hammering

Fig. 10

Soldering

Fig. 11

by means of heat alone (see Fig. 13). Stones can be mounted, with bezels or with prongs, and other items or materials, such as niello or enamels, can be used for surface decoration.

You can do almost anything to your silver, except to hammer it so fiercely that you crack it, or use heat so consistently high that you burn holes in it (unless you *want* to burn holes in it). You may find, as you experiment, that you can do things that have not been suggested. After all, someone had to taste the first oyster!

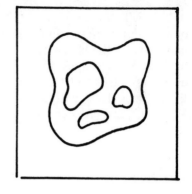

Soldering **Fusing**

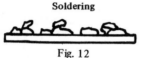

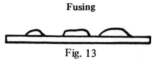

Fig. 12   Fig. 13

As often it is used by itself, and beautiful as it is alone, silver is probably used more often as a frame for a gem-stone. Centuries ago almost all stones were precious, being rare and beautiful, as well as costly. But, today, only four stones—diamonds, rubies, emeralds and sapphires—are considered precious. Semiprecious stones are much less expensive and offer colors of the rainbow for your chosing: the greens of jades, malachite, turquoise, chrysoprase and moss agate; the blues of lapis, labradorite and aquamarine; yellows in citrine, cat's-eye, topaz and amber; pink rhodochrosite, rose quartz and coral; red in garnets, jaspers and spinels; brown smoky quartz, black obsidian, white of pearl or moonstone. Agates and jaspers have all manner of color combinations and marking, some like landscapes in the rock. And you will find it hard to decide which you want first, and harder still to stop before you have bought enough stones to last you for a life-time of jewelry-making. Tumbled stones will cost only pennies, but if you fall in love with amber (and who doesn't?) you can spend a small fortune on a sizable piece with unusual color. Still, somewhere in-between, you're sure to find a color and size to suit your purpose, your taste—and your purse. On page 220, you will find a list of stones by color, with notations to make it easier to choose the stone for your purpose.

You will find it easier to start with a cabochon-cut stone, or one cut with a rounded "cushion" top, to show off the markings or the sheen of the gem. They are usually round or oval, but odd shapes do turn up, either to show off a pattern of markings, or to fit a special design for mounting the stone. Look for a stone with a flat base—it makes for easier setting. Most of the agates and jaspers, turquoise, cat's eye, and the star stones (ruby and sapphire), real and man-made, come with cabochon cut. Stones that call for pronged settings (although cabochons can also be pronged, they do not require this kind of mount) are usually cut with facets. This means that small level "faces" or planes (the number varies with the style) are cut into the stone to catch and reflect the light, magnifying the color and depth of the jewel. You always find diamonds cut this way. So are rock crystal, spinel, zircons, most of the translucent quartz family of stones, and "old-fashioned" garnets. The prongs lift the stone off the body of the piece, and permit the light to bounce off the angles formed by the facetting (see Fig. 14).

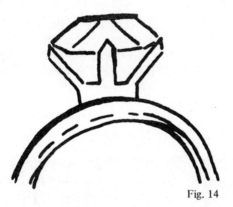

Fig. 14

In addition, there are any number of "found-objects" to set in silver. Beach stones, shells, coral branches and chunks, odd bits of wood, artifacts from past times—arrow-heads, old coins, antique buttons—bits of uncut and unpolished stone crystals, slices of bone or horn, and anything else that appeals to your imagination can be used as part of your creation, and caged, pronged, bezeled or wrapped in silver (see Fig. 15).

21

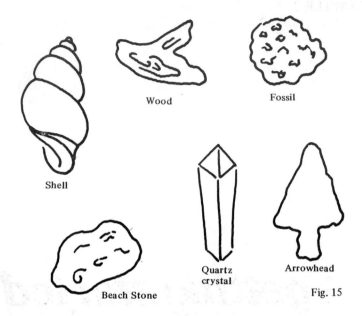

Shell

Wood

Fossil

Beach Stone

Quartz crystal

Arrowhead

Fig. 15

You will learn to use most of the techniques mentioned in this chapter both separately and in combination. Above all, you will learn that being an amateur differs from being a professional in one way only: you are working for *love*, not for money. It does NOT mean that your standards for acceptable work need be lower. You will delight in your creations, wearing them proudly, or using them as gifts, appreciated all the more because they are personal as well as beautiful.

In addition, you will learn to use your eyes creatively. And you will learn, too, that however you use it (and sometimes, even if you abuse it) silver is a wonderful material!

CHAPTER 2

getting started

Your first consideration is your work-area. You're the lucky woman if you have an extra room, a basement corner or a spot in the playroom where you can set up a permanent work-bench. If space is limited, a folding bridge table or the kitchen table will provide sufficient work area. The bridge table (but it must be a sturdy one) has the advantage of put-away-ability. A good piece of furniture should be protected. Everyone has an occasional accident. The most practical protection is a thin sheet (¼") asbestos board, which is the ideal safeguard against flame as well as from saw and hammer marks. It is also easily stored.

One of my friends works at a table on rollers in a crowded apartment. Equipment and tools and boxes of material store on the shelves and the whole thing rolls out of the way into a corner. Another friend has set up a piece of plywood extending out from a radiator in her bedroom on two metal legs, and works there. I find that, more often than not, I am sitting on a step-stool, using the top of a wooden bar stool as my table. Where you work depends on the space available and where you are most comfortable. You will find your own nook.

Two things you should remember: ventilation and light. Your ventilation should be good. This does not mean using commercial vents or blowers. It does, however, mean air space—especially when you use the soldering torch and pickling compound. These are perfectly safe to use, but I wouldn't advise setting up work space in a closet! The area should also be well-lighted. A small student lamp, preferably with a goose-neck and therefore adjustable, will be easy on your eyes and let you see just what you are doing. Some people like hi-intensity lamps.

Beyond this, there are very few work-shop requirements. You can use a chair, a stool, or even an upturned box, as long as you can rest your feet flat on the floor and can sit comfortably. The table should be suited to your height too, so you don't get a backache from bending over a too-low space.

Storing hand tools is no problem at all. If you have a permanent work space, the tools can be hung on a peg-board, in sight and readily available for use. There are many clamps, rings and hangers in the hardware store to use for this. If you have to put things away, one of the easiest storage ideas is the "tool roll." This is simply a length of heavy cotton fabric (a yard is plenty), turned up 6″ along the long side, and stitched into a series of narrow pockets, one for each tool. You'll need more room for pliers than for a file, so measure for each tool before you stitch. When this is filled, it can be rolled up and secured with ties or a rubber band and stored in very little space. It has the added advantage of protecting your tools from scratches and from the ever-present air-pollution. You can also use a wooden or plastic tray designed to hold table silver, a fishing creel, conventional tool box, or even a sewing box. The boxes will let you store material with your tools. Small plastic boxes, with divided partitions, are ideal for storing beads, stones to be set, or "findings." You'll find it easier if you don't have to hunt for jump-rings among the ear-wires. A series of cup-hooks or nails driven into a piece of plywood will serve to hang up coils of different size wire.

Stringed price tags are good for making size-labels. As you work, you will find yourself devising ways of organizing your equipment and supplies, and of making yourself comfortable. Only you can do this, because your requirements will be a little bit different from those of any other craftsman.

After you've decided on your work area, you'll have to give thought to design. What you want to know about is applied design—how do you decide what to make when you want to make something?

The cliche that "form follows function" is not always true, but it's not a bad rule to begin with. A ring *must* have a hole in it for your finger or it isn't a ring. So you must decide first how your piece of jewelry is to be used—will it hang, like earrings or a pendant? Will it be sewed on like buttons? Wrapped on like a bracelet? Pinned into place?

When you have decided on the function, the size will usually suggest itself. A tie-tack will be small; a belt buckle will be large; earrings will be light in weight, but a pendant can be heavier. Is the piece to be made of silver only, or will you mount stones, because the size and weights of these must be considered. When you think about size and weight, you must also think about the intended wearer of the piece.

While it is true that very large pieces of jewelry are often in style, no one can wear a piece that feels or looks burdensome. A little old lady looks silly in long, dangling earrings. Imagine a large belt buckle on a fat man. So you must consider suitability to the wearer, and to the occasions when it is to be worn. Large rings cannot be worn with gloves, bangles are out of place on a tennis court, and protruding bits that catch on clothing or the skin are never suitable, however handsome the pattern looks on paper!

So function and suitability will suggest form: size and shape. It is only then that you begin to consider the other elements of design.

Good design has proportion, motion (this does not mean moving parts), variation and unity, to create a form pleasing to the eye. Remember that what you are making is a statement of your personal good taste—your eye is the one to be pleased.

Proportion is important—a large painting requires a large

frame. Balance goes hand-in-hand with proportion, and can be formal, using identical elements, or informal where a large part is balanced by several smaller parts. Draw some lines on a piece of paper. Do you prefer curves to angles? Circles to squares? Do jagged lines make you feel edgy? Cut some random shapes out of white paper and arrange them on a dark background. Do they satisfy your eye? Move them around to make a different pattern. Do the empty spaces ask to be filled? Partly? Completely? With what?

Variation repeats the same form to keep the design from being flat and static. The forms can be identical, but usually should not be. Straight lines can be different lengths, and need not run in the same direction. Circles can be different sizes. Curves can give the same general "feeling" without being exactly alike. This is more interesting.

Motion lies in the use of the design elements: straight lines are quiet, while curved lines have rhythm. Jagged lines are usually disturbing. Lines running in many directions, straight or curved, confuse the eye. Lines that run off the edge pull the eye away from the piece, while converging lines bring the eye in to help create a sense of unity.

Unity is particularly important, since the parts of the design, no matter how they vary, must fit together in a whole. If you use stones, the beauty of their colors and markings deserve attention, and the other parts of the mount should be directed to this emphasis.

You can add color with stones or by antiquing the silver. If you use stones, you must consider the size and shapes of these in terms of suitability, proportion and balance. You can use texture for decoration, or add texture to color. The watchword here is "restraint." When you reach the point where you're not sure if anything else is needed, stop for a good look—you may have already added too much!

You are surrounded by design sources, and your most valuable tool is a "seeing" eye. There's a difference between *looking* and *seeing*—you can look at a thing a hundred times without seeing its basic shape. When you learn to strip away nonessentials to see the proportions and shapes of things, you'll find that you see everything differently, whether you are examining a work of art, a natural object, or even advertising lay-outs. Look at city skylines or wind patterns on sand dunes. Notice the shapes of shadows. Watch the curve made by a bird in flight, or the color spots on the wings of a butterfly. Look at the tracery of lines on a smooth beach stone or a piece of marble. Notice how raindrops change shape as they run down a window pane. Whatever you look at, try to *see* the shape instead of being diverted by the color and the surface decoration.

Start a notebook and carry it with you. Sketch ideas as they occur to you—and how they will—a few rough lines will do to remind you of the pattern. You need not be an artist. Make a simple sketch of the shapes you see around you: flowers, shells, an iron gate, trees. Notice that leaves, even on the same tree, differ slightly. See what a beautiful tracery their veins make. Everything will suggest ideas: the curve of a fat pottery jug or a delicate wine-glass, turned upside-down, might make a lovely pendant or earring. Leaf and flower shapes have been used for centuries as design elements. Sketch the pattern made by the membranes of a slice of orange—or the way the seeds lie in a cucumber.

Start an envelope of clippings. You'll find magazines a bonanza. Cut out pictures of work in other media: plastic, wood, embroidery, other metals. Look at fabric patterns. See how color and dark-and-light masses are used for book covers, bath towels, and dishes. Even commercial trade-marks can suggest design to you. Everything is adaptable. Many of them are adaptations to start with—from nature or from industry. You can use them all as take-off points for your own designs.

Forget about the "I can't draw a straight line" bit. Almost no one can, without the help of a straight edge. But you *can* draw a curved line, and that's much pleasanter to see. You'll find that you prefer some shapes to others. That's quite all right. In today's world conventional shapes are used less than variations on those shapes. The circle may be flattened slightly; the oval can become an irregular tear-drop. The shape you use is less important than what you do with it. As you use your eyes and your hands, you will develop confidence in your own good taste.

Just remember—when in doubt, keep it simple!

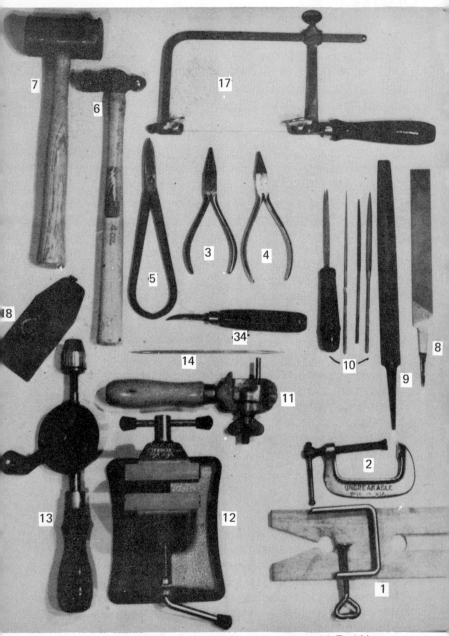

Plate 2A: Basic tools—(photo I)—check numbers with Tool List.

28

your tools & how to use them

Following, you will find a list of tools. Some you will need to buy; others you can make or borrow, and some you can dream about. You need not buy them all at once. Your first projects require very few tools, and other items can be added to your work bench as you need them. The number before each tool is its List Number, by which you will find it in the photos at the beginning of the chapter and by which it is listed under each project.

Plate 2B: Basic tools—(photo II)—check numbers with Tool List.

Essential Tools

LIST NUMBER
 1 Bench pin and clamp (also called V-pin)
 2 C-clamp
 3 Pliers, round-nose, 5"
 4 Pliers, flat-nose, 5", smooth jaw
 5 Plate shear
 6 Hammer, ball-pein, 8-oz.
 7 Mallet, 2" face, fibre, wood or leather
 8 File, flat, cross-cut, # 1 (medium)
 9 File, half-round, cross-cut # 1 (medium)
10 Needle files, (English — medium) round, 3-square,
   ½-round, and barrette
11 Hand vise
12 Bench vise, small, clamp-on style
13 Hand drill, set of twist drills (fine) cup-hook
14 Scriber-poker combination
15 Tweezers
16 Wire soldering tweezers
17 Jeweler's saw frame, adjustable, 4" throat
18 Saw blades, 1 doz. each, #1 and #1/0
19 Fine-tipped camel's hair brushes
20 Torch, Bernz-O-Matic, small & medium tips
21 Asbestos square, 6" x 6"
22 Wire mesh square, 4" x 4" (nikrome or steel)
23 Magnesium brick, 3" x 6" x 1½"
24 Charcoal block, 3" x 4" (medium size)
25 Jar of "Handy" flux, 1 oz.
26 Iron binding wire, medium fine, 1 spool
27 Sparex (pickle) 1 Pt. powder
28 Yellow ochre powder — small bottle
29 Hard silver solder — 1 strip each of hard, medium, easy
   grades
30 Emery cloth — 1 sheet each: coarse, medium, fine
31 Crocus cloth
32 Steel wool, #2/0 and #4/0
33 Jeweler's polishing cloth
34 Burnisher

NICE-TO-HAVE-TOOLS
(BUT YOU CAN LIVE WITHOUT THEM)

Wooden clamp, or ring clamp
    (for holding small pieces while you work)
Ring mandrel, for sizing and forming ring shanks
Combination bench-pin and anvil
A Third Hand
    (just what it sounds like—for help in soldering)
Parallel pliers
Other pliers: half-round, riveting, forming, etc.
Metal gauge
    (for measuring plate and wire)
A complete set of needle files
Chasing hammer
Side-cutting wire clipper
Aviation shears, straight
    (for cutting heavier metals)
A set of Scotch stones: coarse, medium and fine
    (for cleaning and polishing)
Copper tongs
    (for use with pickle bath)
Stone pusher
    (for setting stones in bezels)
Jiffy Clamps
    (for soldering)

Buying and Caring for Your Tools

Memorize this sentence: Respect your tools. Buy the best you can afford; take good care of them; learn to use them properly. That's the whole thing in a nutshell.

In Chapter 2, the discussion on work space suggested several ways to store tools. I prefer the cloth tool-roll for protection and convenience, with larger pieces (saw frame, mallets, etc.) hung on a peg-board. You may find a box or a drawer suits your situation. Do not let the files heap up. If they rasp against each other the teeth will dull, and they will no longer work well. Do not leave the blade in the saw frame when you are finished: loosening the tension will keep it in good condition. Besides, if you bump the handle accidentally, you'll snap the blade. Wash out your brushes—if they cake they will shed hairs. Keep your tools bright and clean: the hammer's face and the plier's jaws can be rubbed with emery paper when they begin to darken from ever-present pollution. Use each polishing stick (or buff) for one compound only. Cleaning up takes only a few moments, but neglected tools will make your work suffer. I repeat: just as you owe it to yourself to buy the finest tools you can afford, you owe it to yourself to keep those tools in the finest condition.

Go through the list and look at the illustrated tools. If you have a home tool-box, check it to see what you already own. You may be surprised at the goodies you never knew you had! If you can, beg or borrow tools to begin with. After that, check the local hardware shop and dime store because some of the items will cost less there than at a craft supplier. Each project has suggestions for making-do and improvising with ordinary household items.

How to Use Your Tools

We'll now discuss each tool and its specific use. Don't worry about remembering everything immediately. Familiarize yourself first with names and basic functions and then use this chapter as one of your most valuable reference sources. It'll be no time before you'll recognize and understand each tool on your own.

BENCH-PIN (#1): This is your first basic piece of equipment. It is a board and clamp to attach to any flat working surface, with a V-cut from the protruding end. You rest your work on it while sawing or filing. If you are handy, you can cut your own from a ½″ thick piece of maple (a hard wood) 7″ long x 2½″ wide (see Fig. 16). If you make your own, you will need two C-clamps, and you must sandpaper the edges carefully to avoid splinters.

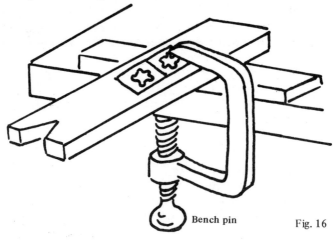

Bench pin   Fig. 16

JEWELER'S SAW (#17-18): This tool must be used properly, since you will use it for every piece you make. It takes a little practice, but is easy once you've got the hang of it. If you look at the plates for Chapter 8 you will see that very intricate designs can be made using only the saw. The frame consists of a wooden handle and several pieces of metal connected with wing-nuts. At the open throat (where you put the blade) there are wing-nuts top and bottom, holding small loose squares of metal against the frame. In order to "thread" the saw, one end of the blade is fastened into the top slot between the metal square and the frame, and the wing-nut is tightened. The blade has a short section at each end without teeth. The teeth of the blade must face *down* and *out* (see Fig. 17). The top of the frame is then rested against the bench-pin or the edge of the table, with the handle resting at right-angles on your body. This leaves both

Fig. 17

hands free to handle the blade and the wing-nut on the bottom of the throat. With your body, you push gently against the handle to decrease the size of the throat while you set the bottom of the blade in place and tighten the nut. When you release your body pressure, you will find that the blade is taut. You can also shorten the throat size by loosening the nut on the back of the frame and moving the base of the frame up a bit. Once the blade is tightened into position, the base of the frame is moved down again until the blade is taut, and the nut re-tightened. Practice threading the frame a few times, until you find the process easy.

The blade is lubricated with wax. You can buy a cake of special wax, but any ordinary candle will do. Run the wax along the sides of the blade—don't choke the teeth.

The blade will cut *only* on the "down" stroke. Blades come in many sizes, from 4 to 1 and 1/0 to 4/0 (for our purposes), #4 being the heaviest and 4/0 the finest. If the blade sticks while in use, you may be using too heavy a blade. Remember that the thinner the metal, the finer the blade should be. You can disengage the teeth, pulling the saw blade back away from the cut (the back of the blade has no teeth) *very* gently so you don't snap the blade, pushing up just a little before you start the saw stroke again. Buy two dozen blades to begin with. Expect to break some—everyone does—even the experts.

Once your blade is threaded and lubricated you are ready to use the saw. The metal to be cut has been marked with a scriber, and this side rests, face up, on the bench-pin, so you can see what you are doing. The piece is held with one hand (do not clamp it to the pin) with the line to be sawed over the open V (see Fig. 18). A few tentative up strokes will cut a tiny nick at the start of the line, but if you are sawing heavier metal, maybe the edge of a needle-file will be needed to cut

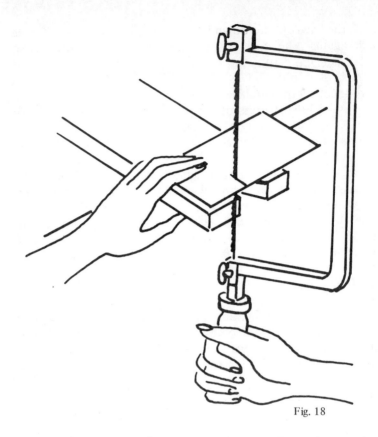

Fig. 18

the nick. Your blade is *always* held at right-angles to the
piece, to cut a straight line and not break the blade. If you
anchor the elbow of your sawing arm against your hipbone,
you'll find that you're quite comfortable, and the blade will
stay in proper position. Don't be surprised when your hand,
holding the handle, bumps your thigh at the end of the
down-stroke. It should. That's a sign that you and your work
are properly aligned to each other.

Your *saw* must do the work. That is, you push the handle
up and down (easy on the up stroke, more firmly on the
cutting down stroke) and the saw will move forward almost
by itself. If *you* push forward you will snap your blade. When
you must turn a curve, you turn the metal piece slowly as
you saw up and down. If you must turn a sharp corner, you

work the saw up and down in place, while you pull the blade back against the edge of the cut (no teeth on the back, remember?) and turn the metal slowly. This is easier than it sounds, as you'll find as you practice. Get acquainted with your local scrap metal dealer. He will sell (or may even give you) small bits of brass or copper plate, wire and tubing, for very little money. On these pieces of scrap metal, scribe curves, angles and straight lines and practice sawing before you work with the silver. You'll be an expert in no time, and, as a bonus, you may find yourself with nice shapes in the other metals that can be combined with silver or each other, or used alone as jewelry.

Saw as close to the line of the design as you can. This means less filing to clean up. Do *not* saw on the line itself. Leave yourself a little extra metal, in case your piece needs adjusting, particularly when you are sawing a frame for a stone or a found object. When you pierce a pattern, you will have to bore a small hole and thread your saw blade through it (make sure the designed side of the metal faces UP) before you fasten the bottom of the blade into the frame. If you push the piece all the way up to the top of the blade, it will hang free while you fasten the bottom nut.

When using the saw, there are a number of don'ts which cannot be emphasized enough. These are:

- Never try to work with a loose blade.
- Never use pliers to tighten the wing-nuts. You will strip the threads. Your fingers will tighten them enough.
- Never set the blade with the teeth facing up (or in toward the throat).
- Never push the saw to the metal; feed the metal to the blade, and turn it slowly as you saw, when you cut a curve.
- Never slant the saw; keep the blade at right angles to the metal.
- Never saw the center 2″ of the blade only — use the whole blade for each stroke. It will last longer.
- Never put the saw away with the blade attached.
- Never tense the hand holding the piece to the V-block, or the hand holding the saw handle, or you'll get a cramp. Relax — it's not that difficult.

PLIERS (#3-4): These come in dozens of sizes and shapes for all kinds of jobs. For your projects only the round-nose and flat-nose pliers (see Fig. 19) are needed. Pliers are used for holding and for shaping. You will hold the end of the wire in the flat-nosed pliers while you manipulate the wire to make sharp angle bends. You will use the round-nosed pliers to make rings on the ends of the wire, and since the size of the nose increases as the jaws meet the handles, you can make many different size rings and curves with the same tool. If you can afford additional tools, get a side-cutting nipper (really a plier) 4½″ size, which can get into spaces that the shears cannot reach, to trim off ends of wire when you've finished bending a piece of work.

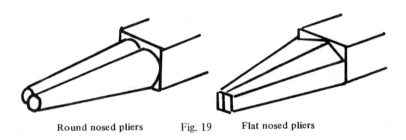

Round nosed pliers   Fig. 19   Flat nosed pliers

FILES (#8, 9, 10): These are used for cutting away extra metal when a saw is not needed, and for smoothing the edges of the metal, and for truing the shape. The coarser file is always used before the finer file, in order to speed the work. Fine files are useful to remove scratches before polishing a piece. Like the saw blade, the file teeth are set to cut in one direction only, but the file cuts on the *up* stroke (away from you). If your work is resting flat on the bench-pin (see Fig. 20) the stroke you make may be in a downward direction, but it will always be away from you, and you will push the handle of the file so that the cut starts at the point of the file. You therefore will lift the file slightly for the return stroke. The half-round file has teeth on both the flat and rounded sides, and is probably the most useful file for general work. The flat file, laid on the work table, is used as a base on which you rub your fabricated bezel (stone setting) to "true" the bottom before you solder it in place. You use the flat file as a base, too, for rounding off the sharp corners of a piece. Needle files are smaller and can reach into corners and small spaces. Medium needle files are finer than the medium large files. Get into the habit of filing over a piece of paper, so you can save the filings in a small medicine vial. You'll have use for them later.

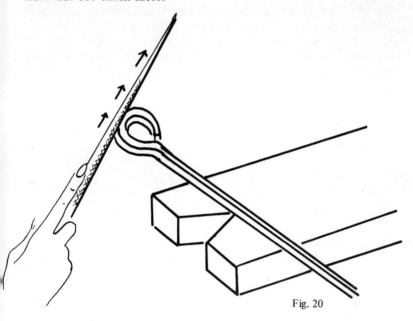

Fig. 20

As with the jeweler's saw, there are several don'ts for using files:

- Never file too steadily in one spot, or you'll wear out a groove impossible to clean up.
- Never file straight across a curved edge or you will distort the shape. File in a "sweep" motion, ahead and to the side at the same time. (It sounds odd, but try it.)
- Never put away clogged files. Rap the edge on the paper to dislodge the filings and save them.
- Never start with a fine file, unless you cannot reach in with the rougher one. Use the fine file for finishing work — otherwise your polishing job will take longer than is necessary.

PLATE SHEAR (#5): This is really a scissors. You will use it for cutting solder into snippets, and for doing rough cut-outs. It will work well on 18- or 20-gauge or thinner metals. For most cutting jobs the saw is preferable.

HAMMERS (#6): These have many uses, and are made in dozens of shapes for specific jobs in silversmithing. For general use, the ball-pein hammer is all you need. This has two faces—one flat, and one rounded (see Fig. 21). The flat is used, with a nail, to make dents for drilling holes. It is also used to flatten metal that has distorted during the work, and for light forging, to shape the metal, or to give it greater strength. For this work you will also need a small block of steel, but the face of an electric iron is very efficient as well. You must aim your blows when you work with the hammer, and use the whole face. The edges will make dents hard to remove. The round head of the hammer is used for texturing with dents (purposeful), and for making the metal dome slightly. Remember, when you use the hammer, you are a craftsman, not a blacksmith.

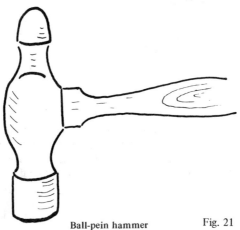

Ball-pein hammer   Fig. 21

MALLETS (#7): These are used for shaping metal pieces, for forming ring shanks and bracelets, when you do not wish to mark the piece. Mallets come with heads made of fibre, wood, leather, rubber and even plastic (see Fig. 22). A 2 or 2½-inch (face-diameter) wooden mallet makes a good brace-let mandrel.

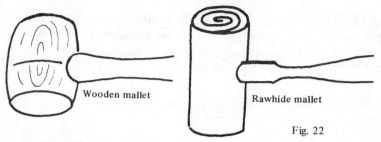

Wooden mallet

Rawhide mallet

Fig. 22

SCRIBER-POKER (#14): Also called a machinist's scriber, this is a 9-inch metal rod, with a bent point at one end (see Fig. 23). This is used to hold the parts together during soldering, and for pushing back into position the snippets of solder that move when the flux bubbles. The other end is used to mark out lines for sawing, or for marking the spots when additional pieces of metal are to be soldered to the base. If solder melts on the end of the poker, file it off, so you don't get a build-up of solder to blunt the point.

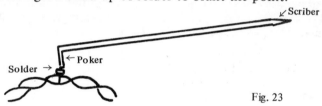

↙ Scriber

Solder → ← Poker

Fig. 23

TWEEZERS (#15-16): These (see Fig. 24) are used for holding pieces of your work when transferring small parts from one area to another, and for holding the work during soldering. The soldering tweezers, which are pressed to open, will lock on the parts to be soldered, and are designed for use with heat. Do not use regular tweezers for soldering because the heat will soften the point and they will distort.

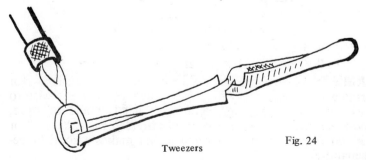

Tweezers

Fig. 24

HAND-VISE (#11): This is a holding tool with jaws controlled by a wing-nut (see Fig. 25). You will use it to twist wires that are too heavy to be twisted with the hand-drill and cup-hook. You can also use it to hold small pieces for filing.

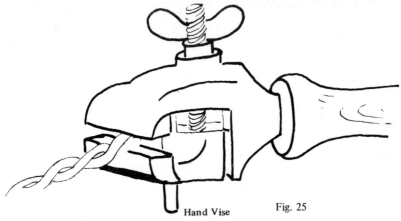

Hand Vise   Fig. 25

BENCH-VISE (#12): This is a truly valuable adjunct. Get one with smooth jaws, so you don't scratch your work. If you have one on a work bench, you can line the serrated jaws with L-shaped removable copper pieces (see Fig. 26) or

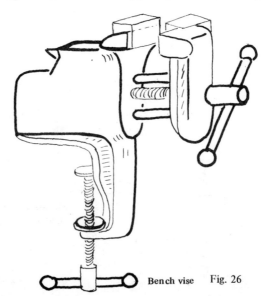

Bench vise   Fig. 26

leather scraps. It takes the place of an assistant when you are twisting wires, because you can anchor the ends into the vise and still have two hands free to operate the hand-drill. You can use it to hold the bezeled ring while you push the bezel edges over the stone you are setting.

HAND-DRILL (#13): The name of this tool describes what it does. Twist drills (sometimes called bits) are locked in the chuck at the bottom of the drill and used to drill holes of varying sizes in metal. You will drill small holes for piercing with the saw, or you can make a design of different-sized drilled holes. When used for boring holes the work should be clamped (using a C-Clamp) to a scrap of soft wood to the work table (see Fig. 27). The spot to be drilled will already have been marked by a nail, hammered gently with the ball-pein hammer's flat face. The drill is always held perpendicular (at right-angles) to the metal. The handle of the drill is rotated rapidly in a clockwise motion to cut the

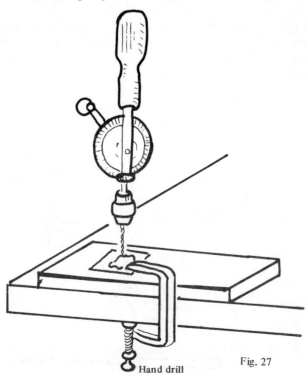

Fig. 27

Hand drill

43

hole, reversed to counterclockwise to withdraw the drill. You must not press down too hard with the drill or you will snap the bit. Twist drills come in 80 sizes—the higher the number the finer the drill and the smaller the hole it cuts. You will use # 52, # 55, # 56 and # 60, which make fine holes.

When you use the hand-drill for twisting wires, you insert a cup-hook into the drill chuck and use that to hold the wire taut (the other ends of the wire are anchored into the bench-vise) while the handle turns it into a twisted rope very rapidly.

TORCH (#20): This is second only to the Jeweler's Saw in importance. It has two basic functions: to anneal the metal or make it soft and workable, and to join pieces of metal together in a permanent bond. Although small pieces of metal can be annealed with a Bunsen burner or even the open flame of a gas stove, the torch is more reliable.

Items #19-29 on the list are all soldering accessories, used with the torch. The **ASBESTOS BLOCK** (#21) protects the work table; the **CHARCOAL BLOCK** (#24) sits on top of it and reflects the heat to the metal. The **WIRE MESH** (#22) and the **MAGNESIUM BLOCK** (#23) are used with the charcoal or in place of it, depending on the job. The **BINDING WIRE** (#26) is wrapped to hold the parts together for soldering. The **FLUX** (#25) is a cleaner and induces the solder to flow. The **BRUSHES** (#19) are used for flux and ochre (one each) which inhibit the solder flow. The **SPAREX** (#27) makes the pickle solution to clean the soldered pieces. It is used instead of the commercial acid solutions which are dangerous to handle.

You are using a Bernz-O-Matic torch designed for home use. The fuel is already mixed, so you have only one knob to turn on, and the flame is easy to adjust. It can be lit with a match, cigarette lighter, or flint-striker. The last is most convenient because it operates with one hand, but the match works just as well. The knob of the torch is unscrewed just a little, so that the first flame is very small. You will use only two of the tips that come with the torch. The medium tip is better for annealing, because it makes a larger, more diffused flame. The small tip makes a fine narrow cone of blue light, and is better used for soldering. If you open the valve too much the match will blow out, but the torch will not light. If you hear a "pop," you have opened the valve too much. Adjust the flame (see Fig. 28) so that it is round, quite full, and shows a little yellow color at the tip. This is a "soft" flame, used to anneal the metal. The metal has been laid on

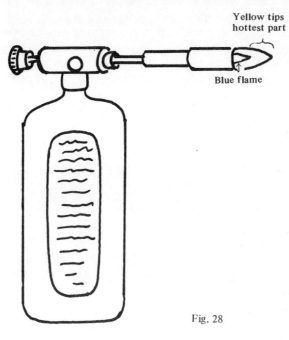

Yellow tips
hottest part

Blue flame

Fig. 28

the charcoal block on the asbestos square. You now move the flame over the metal (do not stay in one spot or the metal will burn) until you see a dull red glow. If you are using a spot-light of any sort, you will see the color better when it is turned off. When the metal glows red, turn off the torch. Pick up the piece with the soldering pliers (#16) or with copper tongs, if you have them. Wave it once or twice in the air before you drop it into a pan of water. Never drop a red-hot piece of metal into cold water—it may crack. Do not pick up a red-hot piece with cold tweezers—it may crack. That is why you set down the torch and turn it off first. The few moments wait is usually enough to cool the metal.

Annealing is necessary when the metal becomes work-hardened (and brittle) when you use a hammer. If you are forging the metal you may have to anneal more than once, to keep it workable.

Soldering is more complicated. Before you start to solder, you must prepare a pan of "pickle," using the dry Sparex powder and water (1 tablespoon of Sparex to 1 pint of water) in a pyrex or copper pan. This will be used to clean the soldered work. **NEVER** put anything into the pickle that is made of iron, tin or zinc. If you contaminate the pickle by touching it with any metal but silver or copper, a chemical change takes place which deposits a coat of copper on your silver that is almost impossible to remove with hand buffing. *Always* remove the iron binding wire before you place the piece in pickle. Use either copper or wooden tongs (or a wooden spoon) to fish out the cleaned piece. (I made a basket from a small plastic refrigerator dish, by piercing holes in the bottom and lower sides with a heated skewer. This is placed in an old pyrex pot that holds the pickle, and since the level of the pickling liquid is always lower than the top of the basket, I can safely use my finger to raise it while the pickle runs out and rinse it with clean water before I must handle the metal. (Sparex will not burn your hands as acid will, but I like to play it safe). The pickle can be used cold or hot—cold just takes longer to work.

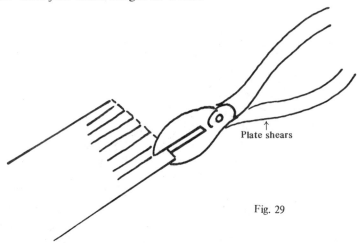

Plate shears

Fig. 29

The second step is to cut the solder (see Fig. 29). Each grade of hard silver solder (#29)—hard, medium and easy—melts at a progressively lower degree of heat. You use them, therefore, in that order for more than one soldering process on the same piece. If you are soldering only once, easy solder will do. (You must not confuse this with *soft* solder, made of lead, which we never use.) The strips of solder are cut into little snippets with the plate shear (#5) by cutting parallel snips into the strip end (see Fig. 30) and then cutting across the first cuts to make tiny pieces, not more than 1/16-inch in size. If you hold the ball of your finger across the bottom of the first cuts, the tiny pieces will not jump all over the place when you cut your cross slices. Cut more snippets than you think you need. They tend to get lost. Keep each strip of graded solder in a separate little medicine bottle, together with any extra bits you haven't used. Mark the bottles so you know what each holds.

If you are going to have to solder more than once, prepare some yellow ochre paste (#28) by mixing a tiny portion of the dry powder with a few drops of water. Use a small jar or bottle cap to mix it. It can be used more than once, by adding water when it dries up. Yellow ochre is a powdered form of earth (used also in oil painting) which keeps solder from flowing where it is painted. You paint it, therefore, over a soldered joint to keep it from unsoldering while you solder

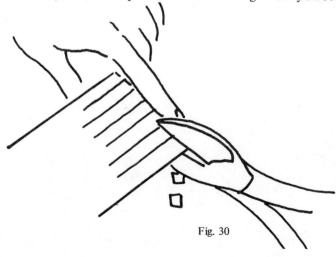

Fig. 30

the next joint. When you become adept at soldering you may not find this necessary, since the next grade of solder will melt with less heat, but on a complicated piece, it pays to be safe. You will also use it later when you want to "ball up" the end of a wire for decorative effect, to be sure that the wire melts no further than you want.

In order to solder two pieces of metal together (or two ends of the same piece of metal) two things are absolutely essential. The parts to be soldered must be clean. Solder will not flow on a dirty surface. This means that you must handle the piece with tweezers, or by the edges, for even the oils from your clean hands can dirty the metal. The steel wool (#32) is used to clean both the metal and the solder strips. The second essential is that the parts to be soldered must fit together tightly, because solder will not fill a crevice or jump a gap. This means that you must file the edges, check them to be sure they line up, and file again, if necessary. (Filing will also clean the area to be soldered). Hold the parts up to the light to check that the fit is tight. Oddly enough, the tighter the fit, the better the solder will fill it. Two flat pieces to be soldered together must be completely flat, or the joint will not be perfect. Binding wire is wrapped around the pieces and tightened with pliers (see Fig. 31) to hold the joined parts stationary during the soldering process. The entire piece

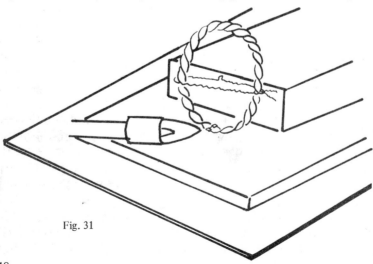

Fig. 31

(not just the joint area) is then fluxed and set into place for soldering. Or it can be set on the charcoal block and then fluxed. The entire piece is fluxed to prevent oxidizing (or blackening) from the heat of the torch. As you set the solder snippets in position with the brush dampened with flux, you will be fluxing them. Only now do you light your torch.

Light it as you did to anneal the metal, and with the same soft flame, dry the flux on the whole piece until it looks like dry white paint. You have placed your snippets of solder across the joint to be made (see Fig. 31) or along the sides of the flat parts. The pieces of solder should touch both parts to be joined. As you dry the solder, the poker (#14) is used to replace any snippets that bubble out of position with the drying flux. Now you increase the flame, until you have a small point, enclosing an inner cone (see Fig. 31). The hottest part of the flame is from the tip of the inner cone to the top of the outer one (see Fig. 28) and this is what you use to solder with. The flame is kept moving constantly, not too rapidly as to be ineffective, but enough so that the flame doesn't burn through the metal, as it will if it concentrates on one spot. Since solder runs towards the hottest point, the larger piece of metal to be joined is heated first. The flux will complete the burning-off process, and the white paint will crack and peel and the silver will show with a glistening white shine. Move the torch in a rotating motion, towards the side of the joint, then back over the piece and around to the other side. If you throw the flame directly on the joint and on the solder you will either burn the metal or make the solder ball up and refuse to flow. You will also burn off the flux too rapidly, before the whole piece heats, and it will permit the metal to oxidize. When this happens you must clean it in the pickle and start over again to solder the joint. When the base (the larger piece of metal) has heated enough, it will begin to show a dull red glow and you can throw the heat on the joint. You will see a bright "flash" as the solder melts and runs in to fill the joint. When this happens, *remove* the heat immediately, and turn off the torch to give the piece time to cool. It takes only a second to have *too much* heat so that you burn the metal. Take the heat away as the solder starts to flow. You can always return with more heat if the flow stops. *Remember:* if you have used binding wire, remove it before you put the piece in the pickle. Don't put the tweezers into the pickle. When the piece is clean, remove it from the pickle (not with iron) and make sure it is completely soldered. If you have gaps, push the parts together tightly and resolder, using a lower grade of solder. If you have used too much solder, you may have to file away the excess, so don't overload. You'll be surprised to see how tiny a bit of solder is needed. When the piece comes out of the pickle it will be a dull white color if it is completely clean. You will have to repeat the process with each soldering step.

You will use your torch to make little granules (balls) of silver to use as decoration. This is great fun to do. You will also use the torch, without solder, for fusing pieces of metal together. You can make many interesting designs with bits of scrap by this method.

The torch has a number of don'ts which you must familiarize yourself with:

- Never be afraid of the torch (although almost everyone is at first). The worst that can happen is that you burn through the metal or melt the wire. When this happens, don't discard the scrap (although the move toward the waste basket is almost instinctive): if you cannot use it later, you can always sell it. So while it is true that you must repeat your work (reason enough for disgust!) have patience. You will learn from your mistakes. If you let the torch buffalo you, you will find yourself withdrawing the heat just at the last moment before the solder flows, and by repetition, burning off the flux prematurely so you have to start over again anyway.
- Never try to solder a dirty piece. Scratch off all signs of oxidation with the scraper.
- Never try to solder an uneven joint—it just won't work.
- Never keep the heat on one spot—keep the torch moving slowly.
- Never use brass or copper wire for binding. The solder will attach them permanently to your work. Iron wire can be pulled off with pliers.
- Never forget to flux the whole piece and dry it slowly.

- Never forget to heat the larger part first. If you heat the small part first, the solder may flow *up* on it, and not down into the joint.
- Never forget to remove the binding wire before you use the pickle.
- Do not touch the pickle with iron or steel implements—only copper or wood.

The remaining items on the tool list (#30-33) are for polishing. They are used to remove scratches and small surface mars, and to give the silver a brighter finish. The **EMERY CLOTH** (#30) is used in the order in which it is listed—coarse first, fine last. #4/0 **STEEL WOOL** (#32) is finer than #2/0, and therefore used after it. The emery cloth and the **CROCUS CLOTH** (#31) are used more easily if they are attached to strips of thin wood, as hand buffs. You can buy these strips, or make them from 11-inch lengths of 1-inch lath, ½-inch thick. The handles are labelled, so you know what you are using, with the name and grade of the cloth, and 6-inch oblongs of the cloth, about 3½-inch wide are wrapped around the stick and stapled along the short side. This way they will stay in place while you are working, but can be replaced easily when they wear. They are either used in the hand, with a filing motion, or laid flat on the work surface, while the piece is rubbed against the cloth. The edges are useful for getting into corners and crevices of the design. The **STEEL WOOL** (#32) is used in a wad for hand rubbing. Check the work as you polish it. If there are deep scratches you will have to use the needle files, across the scratch on the diagonal, to cut away the metal and make the scratch disappear. You will use the needle files too, to work across the soldered joint area, until the soldering line vanishes. Hand buffing takes time and requires patience, but the results are worth it. The **BURNISHER** (#34) is used to push the bezel wire down around the mounted stone without marring the metal. It is sometimes used for polishing too. The **POLISHING CLOTH** (#33) is two pieces of fabric sewed together. The dark portion is impregnated with rouge for the final shine-up, and the lighter section is to protect the piece from finger marks in the final finishing.

Now let's get to work!

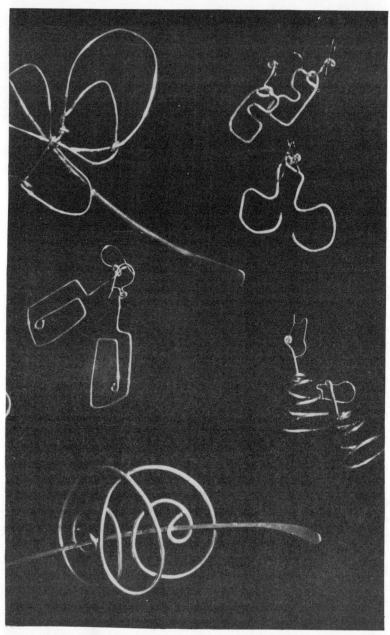

Plate 3: A few of the shapes silver can assume.

bent. *wire*

For your first project, you are going to make a hair ornament that is both a beautiful and useful piece of jewelry. One advantage of this project is that it will help you get the feel of the metal. Your hands will signal that the metal is responding as you want it to. They will indicate when the metal is growing stubborn and needs to be annealed (see Glossary) and made workable again. Since most of the wire you buy is already soft, you can work until it begins to feel stiff. At that point, you can anneal it with the torch or in the flame of a gas stove until it has a soft rosy glow (See Chapter 3). Once you quench it in cold water, it is ready for further working.

Hair Ornament

MATERIALS:
For ornament, one 30-inch piece 14 gauge round wire
For "arrow," one 6-inch piece 14 gauge square wire

TOOLS:
Ball-pein hammer (#6)   Emery cloth No. 1 (#30)
Flat-nose pliers (#4)   Polishing cloth (#33)
Half-round file (#9)

Numbers refer to tools as identified and discussed in Chapter 3.

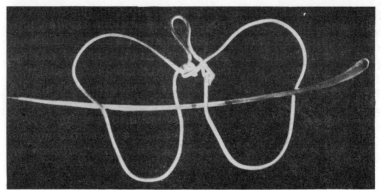

Plate 4: This "butterfly" is a variation of the basic figure-8.

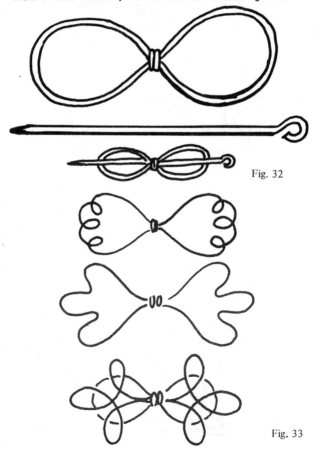

Fig. 32

Fig. 33

54

STEP 1: The basic shape of the hair ornament is a figure-8 with a few extra curls. (Note that a plain figure-8 requires only a 16-inch piece of wire.) The arrow secures the ornament to the hair by passing through the open spaces on both sides (see Fig. 32). The basic shape can be complicated by any number of curves or curlicues (see Fig. 33), just remember that the more elaborate the design, the longer your piece of wire must be. Begin by making curves with your fingers. Leave an inch of wire at either end of the shape to wrap around a touching wire to secure the piece (see Fig. 34).

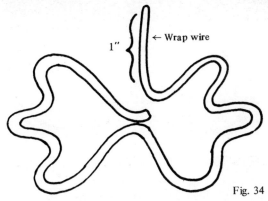

1″ ← Wrap wire

Fig. 34

If you want sharper angles, hold the wire in the pliers and use your free hand to bend the wire firmly, almost as if you were stretching it. Try not to scratch the wire with the pliers as you work to make an easier job of polishing. Once the ends are wrapped and tucked in securely, use your flat-nosed pliers to squeeze the ends as flat as you can get them (see Fig. 35).

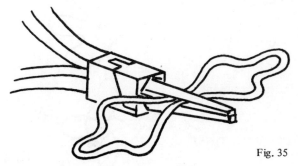

Fig. 35

STEP 2: With the flat side of your half-round file, file the wire ends flat against the touching wire (see Fig. 36) until it feels smooth to your fingers. Remember that your file cuts only on the stroke *away* from you. See that you do not gouge into the other wires with the file as they will be difficult to remove. Set ornament aside.

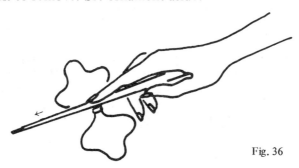

Fig. 36

STEP 3: You are now ready to point the end of your "arrow." Use the file for this too, turning the square wire so that the tapering is even. Start the taper about 1½" from the end (see Fig. 37), working over a piece of clean paper. (Collect the filings and save them, you'll find that they are valuable in later projects.) The finished point should be gently rounded so that you do not get scratched when pushing it through your hair.

1½"

Fig. 37

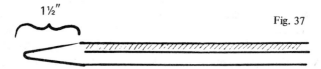

STEP 4: Lay the raw end of the arrow on a clean piece of steel. Hammer lightly with the flat face of the ball-pien hammer (see Chapter 3) until the end has spread into a pleasing shape. It need not be completely regular and can be roughly round or oval (see Fig. 38). Use even blows of the

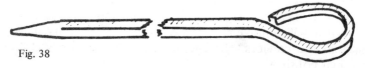

Fig. 38

hammer, aiming them to glance off the edge of the metal. Remember that the metal moves in the direction of the blows, so once it is flattened a little, you should work from the center to change the shape. You may find it less tiring to work from the forearm and not from the shoulder. If you prefer, you can simply bend the end of the wire into a circle or oval and skip hammering the shape.

STEP 5: When you are satisfied with the arrow shape, file the edges smooth. File first from the top of the piece, using a downward push (hold the piece flat on the bench-pin near the edge so you do not catch your file on the wood) and remember to lift the file for the return stroke (see Fig. 20). When the top feels smooth to the touch, turn it over and repeat filing from the bottom. This will give you a slightly rounded bevel edge.

STEP 6: Hammer the length of the square wire lightly to stiffen it. Hammer your main shape *very* lightly. You do not want to dent or nick the wire, just to give it a little body.

STEP 7: Now use the emery cloth to rub both pieces until they shine. The cloth (see Chapter 3) can be torn into small squares more comfortable to work with than the full sheet. You will have to rub hardest over the scratched areas. If the scratches are very deep, you may have to take your barrette needle file and file gently across the scratch to remove it. Check your work frequently and be patient. Polishing can be tedious, but the results are worth it.

STEP 8: A brisk rub with fine (#0) steel wool should give you a sparkling surface. Be careful not to bend your piece out of shape. Washing in warm soapy water with an old toothbrush will remove any bits of emery or steel that have lodged in the crevices. Dry well and use the jeweler's cloth for a final polish.

STEP 9: Hold the piece in the cloth and gently bend the "wings" of the figure-8 away from you so they conform to the shape of the head (see Fig. 39). Try it on to be sure that it will rest comfortably in place. Bend to adjust if necessary.

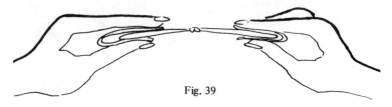

Fig. 39

Variations on the Theme: Pendant

The technique is exactly the same for this first variation, except that the basic shape is that of an egg instead of an eight. Like the Hair Ornament, its shape can be plain or fancy (see Fig. 40). Only one piece of wire is used and the eye for the chain or ribbon is part of the piece itself.

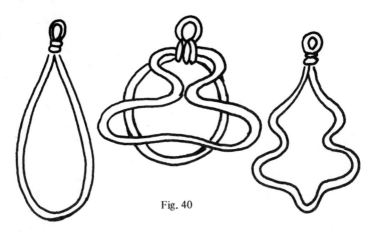

Fig. 40

MATERIALS:
One 18-inch piece 14 gauge round wire

TOOLS:
Same as for Hair Ornament

58

STEP 1: Start to bend the wire for your basic shape about 3½" from the end (see Fig. 41). This will leave enough wire to make your "eye" and wrap the wire securely into place. You can thread the wire back and forth across the curve or weave it between the curves. You can wrap it around itself at any point, either to hold it in place or to make the design trim. Try to end your pattern at the top of the egg shape. If you do this, the wire from the other end can wrap the eye and make the end snug. When you have finished wrapping the wire and secured the end flat with your pliers, grip the "eye" between the jaws of the pliers and twist it to form a right-angle with the body of the piece (see Fig. 42). When your ribbon or chain passes through the eye, your pendant will hang properly.

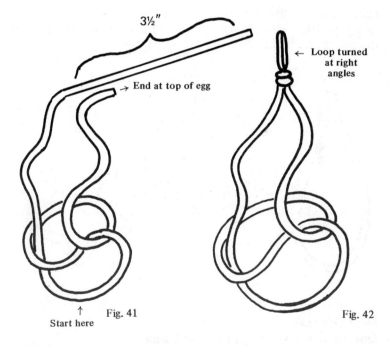

3½"

← Loop turned at right angles

→ End at top of egg

↑ Fig. 41
Start here

Fig. 42

STEP 2: Repeat Step 7 of Hair Ornament.

STEP 3: Repeat Step 8 of Hair Ornament.

59

Finger Ring

MATERIALS:
One 12-inch piece 16 gauge round silver wire

TOOLS:
Same as for Hair Ornament,
  plus a ring mandrel (or a piece of pipe or dowel)

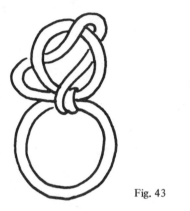

Fig. 43

STEP 1: The preliminary step for the ring (see Fig. 43) is a little different because you must first measure your ring size. Cut a strip of paper ¼″ wide and try it around your finger, marking carefully where the size fits (see Fig. 44). Make sure you can slip it off over your knuckle. Cut away the extra length and mark the paper with your name and which finger and hand you measured—you may want to make rings for other fingers and other people—so you should have a handy

Fig. 44

reference. If you have a ring mandrel, wrap the paper in a circle and slide it on the mandrel to discover your ring size. If you have neither a mandrel or a pipe of the correct size, check your kitchen drawers. (I use an old pancake turner with a tapered round handle that gives me a choice of several ring sizes.) If you use something like this, make an ink mark, so you will know where to position your work. If you have absolutely nothing to work on, you can make your ring shank right on your own finger, then remove it to do your patterning.

STEP 2: Bend your ring shank and twist the ends of the wire first at right angles to each other, then back in the other direction so that the circle for your finger is locked into place (see Fig. 45). You can start in the center of the wire to make the shank, or begin your curve several inches away from one end. This is to leave wire for wrapping securely.

Fig. 45

STEPS 3-8: Once your shank is secure, repeat Steps 1, 2, 3, 6, 7 and 8 of the Hair Ornament.

Earrings

MATERIALS:
Two 5-inch pieces 18 gauge round wire; ear wires, (If you do not have pierced ears, get screw back findings with a tiny loop attached.)

TOOLS:
Same as for Hair Ornament

61

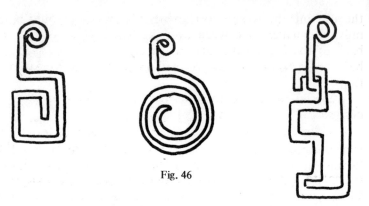

Fig. 46

STEP 1: Start by making a small loop at one end of the wire for hanging the finished earring (see Fig. 46). Make it as small as possible. If you are using screw back findings, bend your own loop at right angles to the earring shape so that it will hang properly (see Fig. 47).

STEPS 2-6: Repeat Steps 2 and 3 and 6-8 of Hair Ornament for each earring.

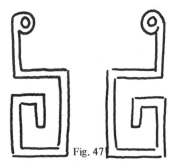

Fig. 47

Design Interlude

When you make bent wire ornaments, the flow and motion of the design creates itself under your fingers, but proportion and balance are very important. With the Hair Ornament for example, the spaces through which the arrow will pierce should be in the top half of the piece, to prevent the entire thing from overbalancing. The size should be in proportion to the use and the wearer—ornaments for children would naturally be smaller—one worn over the forehead instead of the back of the head would also be smaller. The design need not be exactly balanced, but you will probably find this easier at first.

When in doubt, keep it simple. This applies to *all* your designs and can never be repeated too often.

Doodle on paper first, if you like. It may give you more confidence in your ability to make a design. If you scribble on paper use a second sheet with a 2″ cut-out in it as a frame to isolate a portion of your scribbling for a design. Go over the lines you have chosen with ink or red pencil and see if you want to alter or add to them. Use this to work against when you start to bend the wires. Even if you start with a set pattern, you may change it when you begin to play with the metal. Feel free to do this.

Think of your wire as a fence, enclosing space. The sizes and shapes of the empty spaces should echo but not duplicate each other. Look at some of the designs sketched in Fig. 33 for suggestions.

Always be ready to experiment. With bent wire the design possibilities are endless. You might make a series of small figure-eights in 18 gauge wire (2-inch pieces take about six inches of wire each) to thread on ribbon or leather for a belt or a bracelet (see Fig. 48). (You will need about 12-15 for a belt, depending on the size, and three for a ribbon bracelet.) You might try to combine metals, too, using a thinner gauge copper or brass wire to twist with the heavier silver wire. There is a form of brass, with a lovely gold color, called Nu-Gold, available from craft suppliers, for very little money. Don't over-do. Each metal has its own special beauty and will show off to best advantage if your design is simple.

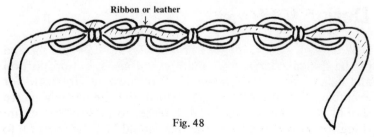
Ribbon or leather

Fig. 48

Plate 5: Single- and double-whorled units can be combined in many ways.

unit con- struction

No one knows where or when the single whorled pattern originated. It has been found at ancient sites as far apart as Scandinavia and Mexico. The earrings which follow consist of two whorls of fine wire, attached to each other without jump rings. You'll find them very easy to make.

Earrings

MATERIALS:
One 22-inch piece 20 gauge round wire
One pair ear wires or screw-backs with ring attached

TOOLS:

Round-nosed pliers (#3)	Torch (#20)
Flat-nosed pliers (#4)	Pickling solution (#27)
Plate-shear (#5)	Dish of clean water
Flux and brush (#25 & 19)	Flat button, about one inch
Asbestos square (#21)	in diameter, preferably
Charcoal block (#24)	of metal
Half-round needle file (#10)	Steel wool (No. 4/0) (#31)
Hammer and nail (#6)	Medium emery cloth (#30)
Mallet (#7)	Crocus cloth (#32)
Hand drill & bit No. 54 (#13)	Rouge cloth (#33)
Hand vise (#11)	

Numbers refer to tools as identified and discussed in Chapter 3.

STEP 1: Turn the button over and remove the little shank, twisting it loose with the flat-nosed pliers. Use pencil and several crossing diameter lines to find the center of the button, and tap lightly with hammer and nail (see Fig. 49). Tap very lightly if it is not made of metal, for you do not want to crack it. Tighten the drill bit into the chuck of the hand drill, clamp the button to the V-pin and drill a hole in the button. (If you have selected a button with holes, skip this first step.)

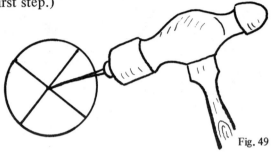

Fig. 49

STEP 2: Wrap the wire around your hand to form a small coil (see Fig. 50). Paint it lightly with flux, and lay it on the charcoal block. Anneal it by moving a soft flame (one with a yellowish tip) around the coil until the flux dries and then turns brownish, bubbles and burns off. Keep the flame moving so you do not burn the wire. You may see the silver begin to take on a rosy glow, but even if you don't, the wire will be annealed when the flux has all burned off. Remember not to hold the tip of the flame too close to the wire. Take a little more time, it's safer. When the flux is gone, drop the coil into the pickle solution. Turn off the torch. When the silver turns white in the pickle, remove it to clean water, then dry and straighten the wire with your fingers.

Fig. 50

STEP 3: Cut the wire into 4 pieces. Two should each be six inches long, and two should be five inches long. Thread one of the six-inch wires up through the hole in the button, leaving about ¼ inch at the bottom. Anchor this short end into the hand vise (see Fig. 51). Anchor the hand vise handle in the bench vise, so you will have both hands free to bend the wire.

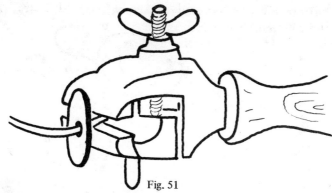

Fig. 51

STEP 4: Use nose of flat nosed pliers to turn wire in sharp right-angle bend, so that it lies on top of the button face. Then use round nosed pliers (at very tip) to make the first coil around the wire where it comes up through the hole in the button. Continue making a tight flat coil until you have made six concentric circles. Be careful not to nick the wires with the pliers as you make the coils. Use what is left of the wire to form a one-and-one-half loop circle (a small ring) also lying flat on the button face (see Fig. 52). Remove from hand vise and set aside. Repeat with the second 6-inch piece.

↑
Button   Fig. 52

STEP 5: Thread one 5-inch piece of wire up through the button hole, leaving ½ inch on bottom end to be fastened into hand vise. Repeat Step 4, making five concentric rings and finishing with a small loop and a half on top. Repeat with second 5-inch wire. These will be the top whorls of the earrings.

STEP 6: Use the tip of the round nosed pliers to curl the ¼-inch end on the larger whorls into a tiny ring and push it into the empty center of the design, on each one (see Fig. 53). Hammer lightly with the mallet to push it flat into place and stiffen the coil slightly. Bend the ½-inch end on the smaller coils with the flat nosed pliers to lay flat against the back of the coil, pointing to the bottom (see Fig. 54). The small ring is the top.

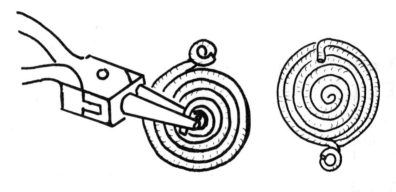

Fig. 53   Fig. 54

STEP 7: Bend the bottom of this end up just a little with the round nosed pliers, hang on it the ring of the larger coil, and close tightly with the pliers to make a one and one-half turn ring (see Fig. 55). Repeat with second set of whorls.

STEP 8: Rub briskly with small steel wool wad, front and back, then with piece of emery cloth and piece of crocus cloth (double it over so you can rub both front and back at once). Use the rouge cloth for a high shine.

STEP 9: Hang pieces on the ear wires or screw-back findings.

Fig. 55

Variations on the Theme: Double-whorled Bracelet

MATERIALS:
16 gauge round wire — 7'8" long
One 7'8" piece 16 gauge round wire

TOOLS:
Same as for Earrings, but omit
  button, hand drill and hand-vise

STEP 1: This is patterned after an original from an Egyptian tomb. First, cut off ¾-inch of wire and use round nosed pliers to form a ring. Use flat needle file if necessary to true the ends for a tight match. Snap closed and set aside.

STEP 2: Repeat Step 1 of Earrings to anneal wire. Straighten it with your fingers and cut it into 14 six-inch pieces, leaving a piece that should be 7¼" long. You will make the double-coils by hand, with the help of the pliers.

STEP 3: Use the tip of the round nosed pliers to make a tiny ring on the left end of one 6-inch strip, and coil, using fingers in *counter-clockwise* motion, to make three concentric rings. Anchor the wire with the flat nosed pliers while you work; you will find it helps keep the coil flat. Repeat, at the other end, coiling *clockwise,* leaving a 2-inch space between coils (see Fig. 56).

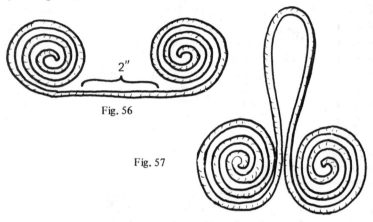

Fig. 56

Fig. 57

STEP 4: Hold the wire so that the coils are on the side nearest you, and pinch the wire at the direct center of the flat area with the tips of the round nosed pliers. Use your fingers to bend each coil in toward the center, moving it on the same plane, not down (see Fig. 57). Pinch the wires together so that the coils touch, side by side. Set aside. Repeat with all 6-inch lengths of wire.

STEP 5: Repeat with 7¼-inch length, which will give you a link with the same size coils, but a slightly longer neck.

STEP 6: Rub each unit with doubled-over emery cloth to clean and polish.

STEP 7: On each piece, turn the neck into a hook by holding the flat nosed pliers across the wire just at the top of the coils and making, first a right-angled turn back, then down against the back but not flat against it (see Fig. 58).

70

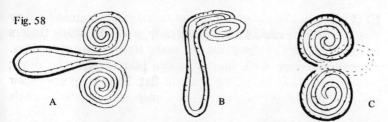

Fig. 58

A   B   C

STEP 8: Assemble, by sliding the jump ring on the hook of the first link. Slide the hook of the first link through the loop of the hook of the second link (see Fig. 59). It will slide in sideways, then straighten out as the narrowest part settles into the loop. Continue with each link in turn, until you have a row of attached links. The hook of the last (the longest) unit will fit into the jump ring hung on the first unit to close the bracelet. When the neck of this last unit has been pulled through the loop of the last regular-sized unit and hooked as all the other units were, it (the hook) is then bent up at the end to form the catch. Try it out on the copper scrap wire: it works very easily.

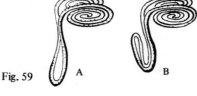

Fig. 59   A   B

STEP 9: Turn whole bracelet over and hammer lightly with mallet to make all hooks same level, so the bracelet will be comfortable to wear. Rub briskly with rouge cloth for a high shine or antique the piece.

STEP 10 (Optional): Antique the bracelet by making up a small amount of liver of sulphate solution in a covered plastic container. Use a piece about the size of your pinky nail in 4 oz. hot water. Place bracelet either flat or coiled into solution for about 30 seconds to darken it. Clean up by rubbing back of bracelet with dampened toothbrush dipped in cleanser. Rub the front with cleanser on your finger, so that you leave all the darkness in the areas between the coiled wires and just shine up the tops of the wires. Do this before you use the rouge cloth.

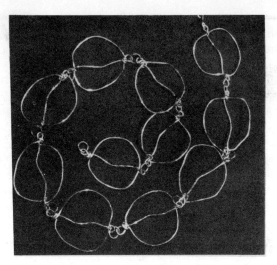

Plate 6: Units made on a jig combined with jump-rings
for an airy necklace.

Necklace

MATERIALS:
One 12-inch piece 20 gauge round wire
One 6-foot piece 18 gauge round wire

TOOLS:
Same as for Earrings plus
  skewer or No. 4 knitting
  needle (to use as mandrel)

Block of soft wood
Handful of headless 2d nails

STEP 1: Make coils of both wires and anneal each coil as directed in previous projects. Straighten out the 20 gauge wire, and form jump rings, by wrapping around a mandrel. (The knitting needle or skewer will make rings ¼ inch in diameter.) Set one end of the mandrel in the hand-vise and tighten in place. With your fingers, wrap one end of the wire tightly around the other end. Next, play the wire out through your fingers, held close to the mandrel, while you turn the hand-vise with the other hand. Be sure the coils are close

72

together and there are no kinks in the wire. You can count the coils to see how many rings you have made, but while you are at it, make extras and use up all the wire as jump rings are always useful.

STEP 2: Thread the saw frame with a fine blade (No. 1) with the teeth facing down and out, and slide the coil off the mandrel, holding it in shape so the rings stay uniform in size. Start to saw where the wire ends, holding the coil in your fingers as you saw. Each ring will drop into your palm or slide on the blade, from which it is easily removed. Without distorting the shape, set the ends of each ring together, holding it up to sight against the light and checking the fit. If you have sawed a clean line, apply tension by moving the ends of the ring past each other a little then gently back again, until you can fit the ends together with a small snap. If there are gaps, insert the flat needle file between the ends, holding the ring with one hand while you move the file back and forth between the ends, thus truing both ends in one motion. Check frequently against the light so you don't file away too much. Apply tension when the ends mate.

STEP 3: Use paper and pencil to make a pattern for a link. It should be a continuous line but not so complicated that it will require an excessive amount of wire (see suggestions in Fig. 60). Make the pattern actual size. Glue the paper to the block of soft wood. Make sure it is smooth. Dry completely.

STEP 4: Make your jig by hammering nails into the wood block *inside* the lines of the pattern. Make sure the nails go in

Fig. 60

Aspen leaf

Initial

Heart

straight. Do not drive them in too far. Put several nails close together around a curve, but one nail alone will hold a small looped curve (see Fig. 61).

73

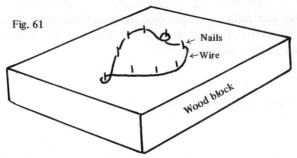
Fig. 61

Nails
←Wire
Wood block

STEP 5: Uncoil and straighten the 18 gauge wire that you annealed in Step 1. With shears cut 11 pieces, each 6-1/8-inch long. Set aside remaining wire. Use the needle file to smooth the ends of all the pieces, and work one piece at a time.

STEP 6: Curve the wire into shape around the nails on the jig. Twist the end into a tight loop. Lift each shape off carefully and set aside until all 11 shapes are made. Use the mallet to hammer each shape flat. The mallet will not mark the wire, but don't beat it to death. Light, even taps (front and back) will flatten it and give it sufficient stiffness.

STEP 7: Open a jump ring (to the side not outward) and use it to connect the bottom of one shape to the top of the next one. Close ring tightly. Continue to do this until you have a row of shapes, beginning and ending with a jump ring. Leave the last ring at one end open.

STEP 8: Make a catch with the wire set aside in Step 5. The one in Fig. 62 is actual size to help you. It should use up less than 1½" of wire. Make the small ring on top tightly closed, and when the shape is made, lay it on a flat surface and hammer it lightly with the mallet, turn over and repeat. Slide the ring on to the open jump ring and close it tightly.

Fig. 62

STEP 9: Use pieces of folded over emery cloth and crocus cloth to polish each link, front and back with one motion. Rub with rouge cloth for a high shine.

NOTE: This necklace will lie just at the base of your throat, but you can make a longer one by attaching more shapes and jump rings. If you make an extra pair of shapes, you will have a pretty pair of matching earrings.

Design Interlude

When you plan a design for Unit Construction, which is a repeated pattern, the important thing to remember is that the units must be joined to each other in a natural fashion.

Each unit, therefore, should include two areas where linkage is inevitable. Although jump rings can be used, as with the necklace, it is better to create a pattern that includes at least one loop that can be connected to the adjoining unit, so that one part of the pattern seems to grow out of the next one.

The denser the pattern (the first two pieces) the more silver you will need to use. The heavier the wire, the larger the unit, and the less silver wire required. For instance, if you made the bracelet with 18 gauge wire you would need 20 6-inch lengths of wire plus one 7-inch length. But you could use 10 gauge wire and use only 36 inches to make a copy of the biceps bracelet worn by Viking chieftains. Eighteen inches of 10 gauge round wire will make a bracelet of this type to be worn at the wrist. You can use 16 gauge wire on your jig to make a handsome belt.

Making jigs and working out patterns for them is great fun. Other suggestions for jigs are included in Chapter 19.

When you have spare time, make up several batches of jump rings in different sizes. A small sectioned plastic box makes a good depository for these, and you can see at a glance the size and number available for use. They form a very important part of almost all forms of jewelry. You will use them to link together bracelet or necklace parts; to hang earrings; or as a pendant hanger. They can also be melted down to make little balls for decorative accents, or soldered or fused to a background as part of the pattern. You can link them together with or without design elements to make chains. They can be made in any size and from any gauge wire, but the most usual choice is 20 gauge round wire.

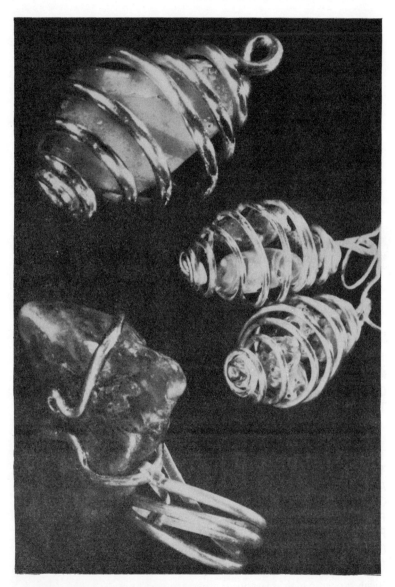

Plate 7: Silver cages for tumbled stones.

cages & wrappings

Pendant

MATERIALS:
One 12-inch piece 14 gauge round wire
Tumbled stone or other object to cage (not more than
  ¾" wide and 1-3/8" long), silver chain

TOOLS:

Torch and medium tip (#20)	Flat-nosed pliers (#4)
Asbestos square (#21)	Half-round needle file
Charcoal block (#24)	(#10)
Flux and brush (#25 & 19)	Steel wool, No. 2/0 (#31)
Pickling solution (#27)	Medium emery cloth (#30)
Dish of clean water	Crocus cloth (#32)
Round-nosed pliers (#3)	Rouge cloth (#33)

Numbers refer to tools as identified and discussed in Chapter 3.

STEP 1: Anneal wire by making a coil and laying it on the charcoal block. Paint with a thin coat of flux and light your torch. Use a soft flame to anneal. This flame is rounded in shape and has a yellowed end. Play the flame on the wire coil and keep it moving around in circles. The flux will first dry almost white, then turn brownish, bubble and crawl as it burns off. The wire will be annealed when the flux has all burnt off. Turn off the torch. Drop silver into pickle solution. When it turns white, remove it (with fingers, wooden spoon or copper tongs) to clean water. Dry and pull wire straight with your fingers. It should not feel stiff at all if it has been properly heated.

STEP 2: Use the tips of the round nosed pliers to make a small ring at each end of the wire (see Fig. 63). The rings

Fig. 63

should face each other and lie on the same side of the wire. Make one ring a little larger than the other. Start at either end and coil the wire around the base of the ring and at right angles to it, using your fingers and the flat nosed pliers across the coil to hold it in place as you bend the wire around (see Fig. 64,A). Make the coil as tight around the base of the larger ring as you can make it. This will be the top of the pendant. Make the first coil of the other end a little looser, because when the cage is finished you are going to push the ring in to fill this space. Continue to coil the ends toward each other. You should have four complete circles in each coil by the time they touch each other (see Fig. 64,B).

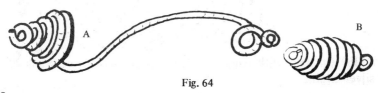

Fig. 64

STEP 3: Use the flat nosed pliers to bend the two coils back-to-back with the two center rings facing outward. Insert the tip of the round nosed pliers into one ring and pull the coil out to form a spiral (see Fig. 65). Repeat with the other ring. Bend the smaller ring back with the flat nosed pliers until it lies flat inside the first coil at that end of the double spiral.

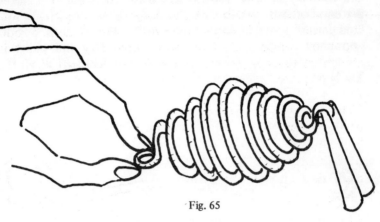

Fig. 65

STEP 4: Rub with steel wool, then with crocus cloth, to clean and polish the cage.

STEP 5: Use your fingers and the flat nosed pliers to open the spiral at the widest part (pull apart like a nutshell). Insert stone or object (see Fig. 66). Close, evening the coil as you do so.

Fig. 66

STEP 6: Rub with rouge cloth for final polish and hang on silver chain.

Variatons on the Theme: Earrings with Beads

MATERIALS:
18 gauge round wire
One 24-inch piece 18 gauge round wire
Six coral or stone beads
One pair ear wires or screw backs with ring
  attached

TOOLS:
Same as for Pendant

STEPS 1-5: Repeat Steps 1 to 5 of Pendant, wrapping three
beads in each cage.

STEP 6: Rub with rouge cloth and hang on ear wires.

Ring with Wrapped Tumbled Stone

MATERIALS:
One 12-inch piece 16 gauge half-round wire
Tumbled stone, not smooth, if possible

TOOLS:
Same as for Pendant plus
  mallet and ring mandrel

Wrapping is another form of caging, but the wire is not
formed into regular coils first. Instead it is placed where it is
needed to hold the stone firmly in place. For this reason
irregular stones are suggested.

STEP 1: Anneal wire as in Step 1 of Pendant.

STEP 2: Decide where the stone will sit on your finger. Try
it in several positions to be sure you like the effect. Then
decide where the wire must go to make the stone secure and

anchor it in the position you want. Use the central seven inches of the wire to wrap the stone, starting at the center point of the wire and using both sides to make your wrap. Use the pliers (either or both) and your fingers to set the wire as close to the stone as you can (see Fig. 67). Use the tips of the round nosed pliers to make small crimps in the wires. This is decorative as well as a tightening device.

Fig. 67

STEP 3: Coil each end of the wire around whatever you are using as a mandrel, twist the last ¼″ over an adjoining wire or over one of the original bends, flatten tightly with flat nosed pliers, and use the mallet to true the ring shank, so it fits your finger comfortably (see Fig. 68).

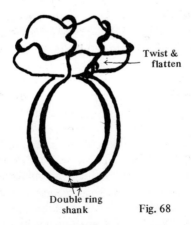

Twist &
flatten

Double ring
shank

Fig. 68

STEP 4: Use needle file to file the flattened wire end flat and smooth. Rub with crocus cloth piece, folded over to rub inside and outside of ring shank at one time. Polish with rouge cloth.

81

Wrapped Shell Pendant

MATERIALS:
One 10-inch piece 18 gauge round wire
One shell with strongly marked curves or
  projections (like a Murex) not more than
  2" long
Silver chain, thong, or ribbon for hanging

TOOLS:

Same as for Pendant plus bench vise (#12)	Hand drill with No. 54 bit (#13)
Hammer (#6)	Epoxy glue

Numbers refer to tools as identified and discussed in Chapter 3.

All sorts of beachcombing finds can be wrapped in silver wire. Beautiful shells have been used for centuries in very elaborate mountings of gold and precious stones but simple silver wrapping is very effective. And ecological too. Shells with strongly ridged shapes are best for wrapping. These include Miters, Murex, Latiaxis, Whelks, Spinkles, Volutes and small Conch Shells. They come in a variety of colors and markings, and their natural beauty makes them ideal objects for personal adornment. The ridges make it easy to make wire wraps. And since you do not need rare or perfect specimens, they should not be expensive to purchase if your opportunities for beachcombing are limited.

STEP 1: Set the shell carefully in the bench vise, open end down, and tighten the vise enough to hold it, but not enough to crush it. Tighten the bit into the hand drill and operate the handle like an egg beater (see Fig. 69). You want to drill a hole in the top of the shell to push the wire through, but you need not drill too deep because when the top is opened up, the wire will pass through the empty space in the center of the shell and out through the bottom opening.

STEP 2: Anneal the wire, as in Step 1 of the Pendant. Straighten, then push one end down through the shell, until it comes out of the bottom.

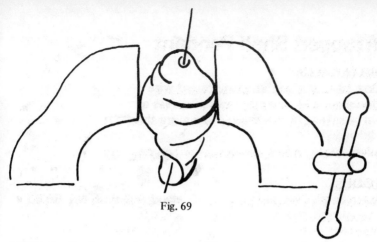

Fig. 69

STEP 3: Push the shell up on the wire so you don't damage it, and lay the end of the wire on your anvil (steel plate or bottom of old iron). Then hammer the last ¼" flat, but don't thin it too much (see Fig. 70).

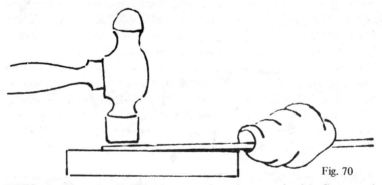

Fig. 70

STEP 4: Use needle file to round and smooth this flattened end. Bend up at right angles to rest of the wire, using flat nosed pliers, slide the shell down to meet bend, and use the pliers to bend the wire up and over the lip of the opening (see Fig. 71). Do it gently, shells are fragile things. This will anchor it in place.

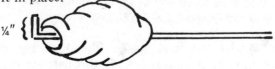

Fig. 71

STEP 5: Use the round nosed pliers to make a ring at the top of the shell, exactly where the wire emerges from the hole (see Fig. 72). Wrap the wire tightly around the base of this ring so it won't pull out of shape, then wrap the wire around the shell, following the natural contours. Make the wrapping as close to the shell as you can, especially as you approach the end.

STEP 6: Where the end of the wire touches the shell, file with half-round needle file to smooth the end of the wire, and taper it flatter on the top (see Fig. 72). Mix 2 drops of epoxy and use it to secure the flattened end of the wire against the shell. Allow it to dry completely before hanging it on a chain, thong or ribbon.

← File & epoxy
here

Fig. 72

Design Interlude

There are two important things to remember when you decide to cage or wrap any object, and wear it as jewelry. The first is that the silver wire should look natural—as if it grew as part of the object. The second is that you must not use the wire so that it obscures the markings or the shape which gives the object its own beauty. Silver cages are most effective for stones or objects with deep or bright color, but relatively few markings, because the markings will be hidden by the coils of silver. Wrapping, on the other hand, can give emphasis both to markings and irregularities in shape.

With these two basics in mind, you can cage or wrap anything. In addition to the items already suggested, think also of pine cones, polished horn or bone, ivory or amber, exotic fruit or plant seeds, balls of other metals, glass beads in all kinds of color and shapes, including the patterned "African Trade Beads." Uncut crystals and rough specimens of gem stones lend themselves beautifully to wrapping, and exotic necklaces have been made from the dried vertebrae of fish!

Consider the size and weight of the object in conjunction with its use. Earrings should be made with smaller, lighter objects than a pendant. But even a pendant should not be so heavy or so large that the wearer is conscious of it. Don't forget that you are adding the weight of the silver wire and the chain or finding to the object itself.

Think of the shape when you want to make a wrapping. If the projections are too angular or too sharp (or too fragile) the wearer will not be comfortable. Some forms of quartz, like Aragonite, are beautiful, but would catch on clothing and pull apart easily.

Twenty gauge wire is usually strong enough for earrings, and is good for a series of small cages to be made into a necklace. Sixteen or 18 gauge is better for rings, but make a double shank if you use 18 gauge. Eighteen, 16, or 14 gauge are all good for pendants. Use 16 or 14 gauge for a hair ornament with a centrally wrapped object.

There is one more type of setting that might be considered either wrapping or prongs, but really is neither one. For this, thin plate silver (20 gauge) is cut into an irregular shape, echoing the shape of the object to be mounted, but with long pointed projections which are rolled around the nose of the round-nosed pliers, close to and over the edge of the object. The Bola Slide in Chapter 14 was made this way. It is a popular method in the making of "Western Style" jewelry. Since it has a bulky look, it is most effective in pieces for men.

Plate 8: Easy-to-make stamped designs.

stamped patterns

This is one of the easiest jewelry projects, and one of the most fun, because you can do so much so quickly.

The first thing to do is make a collection of things to use as stamps. American Indians make their own stamps from large steel nails. After they saw off the point, they file the end into any one of a variety of shapes. You could do this, but it would take a great deal of time. You could buy a set of punches and stamps, but you can also find many things at home that will do a good job. You are looking for objects of metal (not aluminum or lead or other soft metals) that will mark your silver base under hammer pressure, without losing their own shapes. The bracelet pictures at the beginning of this chapter was made by using a screwdriver for the short straight lines, a chisel for the longer straight lines, a small piece of steel pipe for the center circle, the unpointed end of a bolt for the small circles, and the flattened end of a nail for the mark entering each circle. Try out your collected bits on the piece of scrap metal to be sure of the cut each one marks with. You might even saw a section away from a piece of pipe for a curved line. One smart blow of the hammer should be enough to mark the base. If you strike too hard you're likely to punch holes right through the metal. Try to combine some of the marks or repeat them close together for a composite pattern (see Fig. 73).

↑ ↑ ↑   Fig. 73
Nut nail   Bolt head
head

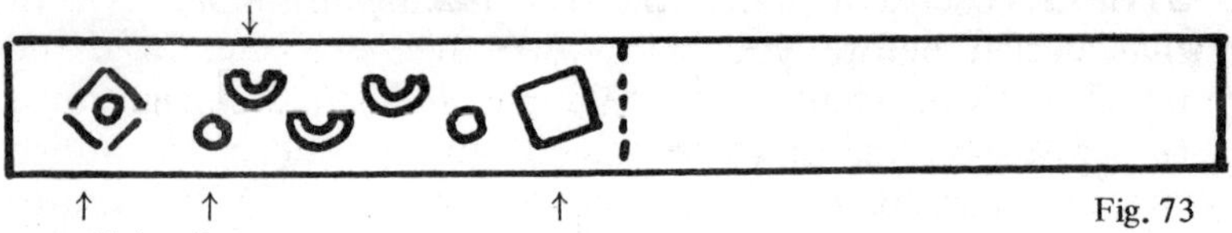

A Textured Open Bracelet

MATERIALS:
One Strip 18 gauge silver, 6″ x 1¼″
One strip 18 gauge scrap copper or brass, any size

TOOLS:
Ball-pein hammer (#6)
and collection of things to
hammer
Mallet (#7) and something
to use as a bracelet mandrel,
old baseball bat, rolling
pin, piece of pipe 2″ in
diameter
Metal plate (or old iron)
Half-round file (#9)

Needle files (#10)
Scriber
Liver of sulphate (optional)
Pumice powder or cleanser
Tooth brush
Fine emergy cloth (#30)
Steel wool No. 2/0 (#32)
Crocus cloth (#31)
Rouge cloth (#33)

Numbers refer to tools as identified and discussed in Chapter 3.

STEP 1: On a piece of paper, outline your bracelet blank, draw a center line and make half a pattern, using the marks you have decided on. You are making only half the pattern to be sure that both halves are identical. When you are satisfied with your design, fold the paper on the center, with the blank side on top and rub over the back with a pencil to transfer the pattern. Open the paper and go over with a sharp pencil to make the entire design distinct.

STEP 2: Attach designed paper to the bracelet blank with rubber cement. Dry completely.

STEP 3: Use each punch in order, making all the marks with that design before you start with the next one. Hold the punch with one hand, at right angles to the metal, right over the corresponding drawn shape and hit the top of the punch with a smart blow of the hammer (see Fig. 74). Be sure to hold the punch down tight against the paper. If you angle it, it may skid under the hammer and mar the silver. Repeat with as many punches as are necessary for your pattern.

Fig. 74

STEP 4: Soak the pattern off the metal. Dry. Check the design on the silver. If any of the marks are incomplete or indistinct, repeat Step 3 directly on the metal.

STEP 5: With the scriber draw slightly curved corners at both ends of the blank (see Fig. 75). Make sure all the corners are even. Use the flat side of the half-round file to remove the extra metal down to the line you have drawn. File carefully (save your filings) so that you don't overrun the line. If you rest the blank on your V-pin, with the corner to be filed extending a little over the edge, you will be able to file (down strokes but away from you) with long firm strokes and cut away the excess metal quickly. Remember to have the light angled so you can see the line where you will finish.

Fig. 75

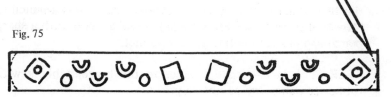

89

STEP 6: With your needle file (also half-round) bezel the edges of the entire blank, by filing gently, with a curving down stroke to remove all the burrs left by the coarse file (see Fig. 76). Turn the piece over and repeat from the back so that you end with smooth edges and slightly rounded ones all around the blank.

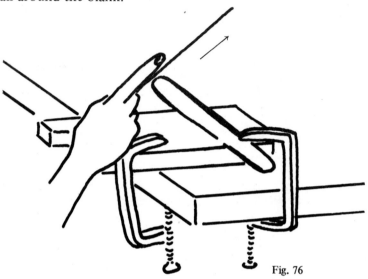

Fig. 76

STEP 7: Remove any surface marks with steel wool.

STEP 8 (Optional): Antique the piece if desired. To do so, dissolve a small (approximately ½″) lump of liver of sulphate in four ounces hot water in a covered plastic dish. Place the blank in this until the silver darkens—30 seconds is enough. Remove and rinse with clean water. Store the liver of sulphate solution in a closed jar for future use. Dampen the toothbrush, dip in pumice powder (cleanser) and rub away the antiquing from the smooth parts of the design, leaving the depressed areas dark. Clean well, rinse and dry. Check the inside to make sure it is also clean. Rub with steel wool until the silver begins to shine again. Polish both back and face of the blank with the usual steps, using the emery and crocus cloths. As you polish make sure not to rub so hard that you take out the antiquing.

STEP 9: Using the mallet and bracelet mandrel, shape the blank to fit your wrist, taking care that the mallet does not mark the metal (see Fig. 77).

STEP 10: Rub the entire bracelet briskly with the rouge cloth, for a high shine.

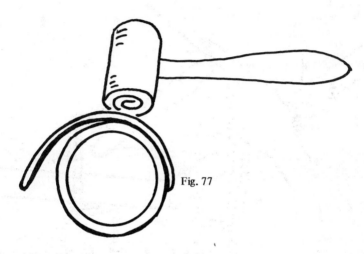

Fig. 77

Variations on the Theme: Textured Spiral Ring

MATERIALS:
One strip 18 gauge silver, 2½"-3" x ½" (the length
 depends on ring size and how much overlap you would like)

TOOLS:
Same as for Bracelet

STEP 1: With a scriber, mark ends of ring blank with a very shallow curve on the top of the left end and the bottom of the right end. Mark a deeper curve on the bottom of the left end and the top of the right end (see Fig. 78). Extend the lines to meet, making the center of the blank a little narrower than the ends will be.

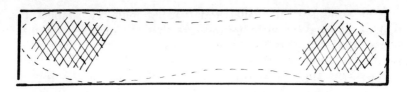

Fig. 78

STEP 2: Use your half-round file (flat side) as in Steps 5 and 6 of the Bracelet to cut away the excess metal and smooth the edges all around the blank.

STEP 3: Repeat Steps 1-4 of Bracelet, choosing punches that make smaller marks. Place your design concentration at the two ends. About ¾″ of pattern at each end is all you need. The rest will circle your finger.

STEP 4: Repeat Steps 7-11 of Bracelet, using a regulation ring mandrel or a dowel stick with the mallet to form the ring. Adjust the size to your own finger. The open ends, where you have placed most of the pattern, should lie on top of your finger.

Design Interlude

This very primitive form of decoration can be combined with other decorative techniques. The Indians usually do this type of patterning around bezeled stones in rings, bracelets, belt buckles and earrings, making the stone the important focus of the design, with the stampings forming the frame. Just remember that a small piece of metal will call for small design parts.

You could form an entire pattern with only a single stamp, if you liked. For instance, the straight line stamp of a screw-driver can be repeated around the entire edge of a piece in one direction and then used in other directions inside this frame. You might also try stamping a central pattern, and then texturing the balance of the blank with light even blows of the ball-end of your hammer. Keep the blows light *and* even or you will distort the metal.

Plate 9: Pendant made with piercing technique.

Plate 10: Sawed-out shapes: small earrings were centers of bracelet links; long earrings were patterned with drill holes.

sawed shapes

If you have followed the sequence of this book, you will already have tried to use the jeweler's saw on scraps of other metals (see Chapter 3). You will need more practice, since you should begin to use the saw even when you think clippers would be quicker: the saw cut is more even. When you are working with a saw, always remember to

- Thread your saw with the teeth pointing *down* toward the handle.
- Lubricate the sides of the blade (see Chapter 3).
- Keep your saw blade at right-angles to your metal and move the metal gently *to* the blade; do *not* push the blade to the metal.
- Let your saw do the work. If you push too hard the blade will snap and you will get a cramp in your hand from tension.

If you remember to rest the elbow of your working arm on your hip-bone for leverage, and use a wrist-and-forearm movement instead of using your whole arm, you will find it much more comfortable.

Earrings

MATERIALS:

One piece 18 gauge silver sheet, 1″ x 2″
   (each earring will be 1-inch square)
One pair of earwires
   (or screw-back earrings with hanging ring)

TOOLS:

Jeweler's saw frame (#17)
No. 1 saw blades (#18)
Half round file (#9)
Barrette needle file (#10)
Hammer (#6)
Nail (to use for punch)
Hand drill (#13)
Paper (for pattern)

Twist drill (with No. 57 or
  No. 58 bit
Rubber cement
Scrap box
Emery cloth No. 1 (#30)
Steel wool No. 0 (#32)
Rouge cloth (#33)

Numbers refer to tools as identified and discussed in Chapter 3.

STEP 1: On a piece of white paper outline the piece of silver. Fold in half to two one-inch squares. Pencil a spot where the earring will hang in one corner of each square. These should be in opposite corners; do not place them too close to the edge or the drill might break the edge later. Also, it should not be too far into the square or the earring will not hang easily. On the rest of the paper, plan your pattern, making curved lines rather than angular ones. Keep your pattern simple and remember that you must saw it out. Don't forget that the finished earring will be diamond-shaped, so plan your design accordingly. When you are pleased with your design, copy it, with a soft pencil, on one of your squares. Then fold the paper so that the blank square is on top of the designed one, and rub the back with the edge of a spoon to transfer your pattern. Cut out the double-designed rectangle and go over the lines carefully. You should now have a small rectangle of paper with two reversed patterns on it.

STEP 2: Using rubber cement, glue your paper rectangle on to the matching silver rectangle. Dry completely.

STEP 3: Using the nail as a center punch, and the hammer, tap lightly on the spot where you marked your corner dot. This will make a small indentation where the drill will enter (see Fig. 79). In the same way, tap a dent *just outside* the line at any point along your design on both patterns. Now clamp your silver rectangle to the wooden V-board with a C-clamp. Insert the twist drill bit into your hand drill, and drill through all four holes.

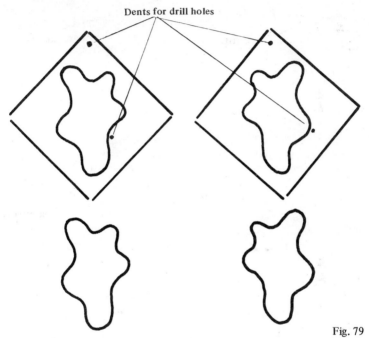

Dents for drill holes

Fig. 79

STEP 4: Thread your saw blade into the top of your frame (with the teeth facing down toward the handle), slide the metal rectangle on the blade through either one of the holes you made along the line of the design, and tighten the blade into the bottom of your saw frame (see Fig. 80). Make sure that the paper pattern faces *up*. Set your work on your V-pin, so that you can anchor it with one hand while you saw. Make sure that your light is angled to make the design completely visible. Be sure that you are sitting comfortably, place tray or paper on your knees to catch scraps. With the

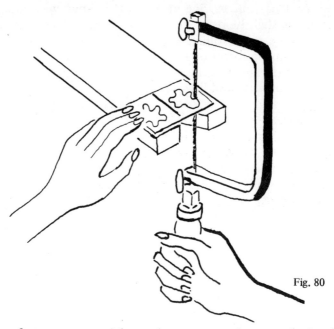

Fig. 80

blade of your saw at right-angles to your piece, work slowly and saw just *barely outside* the line of your drawing. The closer you saw, the less filing you will have to do, and the less silver you will waste. Turn the piece very slowly as you move around the curves. Don't be upset if you snap a blade—even experts do it sometimes. When you have sawed out the first shape, unfasten the blade from the bottom of the saw, slide the piece off and slide it back on through the other hole on the second shape and saw out the second design. Take the whole piece off the saw, and refasten the blade into the frame.

STEP 5: Now saw the whole squares apart. You now have four pieces of silver, two negatives (outlines with the design section removed) and two positives (the sawed-out designs themselves) of the same design. To use the positives, you must repeat Step 3 and make holes with the drill near the top of the shape. If you don't want to make two pairs of earrings now, put the rejected forms in your scrap box. You'll find use for them later.

STEP 6: Place one earring piece on the V-pin, with the edge protruding slightly over the rim. With your hand file, file gently with a small rolling motion. (Remember that your file cuts only in the direction *away* from you.) You are smoothing the edges and putting a little bevel on them. Turn your piece as you work, and lift the file at the end of the up stroke so that you do not accidentally scratch the flat surface of your work. When you have filed all the edges smooth, turn the piece over and file the reverse side. Repeat with the second earring blank.

STEP 7: Cleaning your piece will be simple, if you were careful not to scratch or nick the surface. If there are any scratches, take your barrette needle file, and file gently across the scratches, *in one direction only,* on a diagonal so you do not make the scratches deeper. Check your work as you work, and when the scratches have disappeared, rub with No. 1 Emery cloth until the metal looks smooth. Go back to the needle file if you still see scratches before you use the steel wool. Then rub very gently with No. 0 steel wool for a soft matte finish. Wash well, with warm soapy water and an old toothbrush. Dry. Give a last brisk rub (but don't bend it out of shape) with the polishing cloth for more shine.

STEP 8: Use the round-nose plier to open the small rings on the earring-mounts. Open the ring *to the side,* not outwards, or you will have difficulty reshaping it (see Fig. 81). Slip one end of the ring through the hole in your earring shape and close the rings with your pliers. Repeat with the second earring. If you use a plain earring wire with a little loop at the bottom instead of a ring, just hang the earrings on the wires. Put them on and look in the mirror.

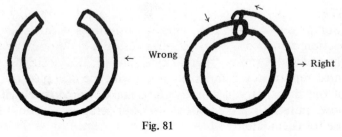

Fig. 81

Variations on the Theme:
Bracelet Threaded on a Velvet Ribbon

MATERIALS:
One 6" x 3/4" piece 18 gauge silver
7-inch piece of ½-inch wide velvet ribbon
Hook and eye

TOOLS:
Same as for Earrings, plus
  needle and thread

STEP 1: Using the same method as for the Earrings, make your own design. Divide the strip of paper into six one-inch links. Along the sides of each line, starting and ending 1/8-inch from the top and bottom, and 1/8-inch in from the sides, draw a line ½-inch long (see Fig. 82,A). This is for threading the ribbon on which the links will sit. Keep your pattern simple (remember the sawing) and make it use up ½" x 5/8" in the center of each link. You may find it more interesting to turn the pattern upside-down for every other link (see Fig. 82,B). Or you can use two separate patterns for variety, if you like. You will find it easy to repeat the patterns if you repeat Step 1 of the Earrings on the first two links, separate that rectangle from the rest of the 6-inch strip, lay it face down on the second two links, transfer the design, and repeat for the last two links.

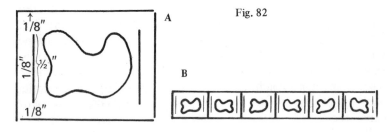

Fig. 82

STEPS 2-6: Repeat steps 2-6 of Earrings *except* that you will need to mark and drill holes *only* near a line of the design on each link, and at the base of each of the lines along the sides.

STEP 7: With your fingers, very gently bend each link away from you so that each one is slightly curved. This will make the bracelet conform to the shape of your wrist.

STEP 8: Repeat Step 7 of the Earrings.

STEP 9: Assemble by stringing the silver links on the ribbon, threading down through the left-hand slit, under the design, and up through the right-hand slit. The bracelet is planned so that you can turn a ¼-inch hem at either end of the ribbon, sew a hook on one end, and an eye on the other. You may prefer to use a longer ribbon and tie it in a knot or a bow. You can make 18 links and space them further apart on a longer piece of ribbon for an unusual belt.

Design Interlude

You find, once again, that curved lines and shapes seem to have more variety, and are softer than angular lines. They have more flow and are easier to balance, because almost any curved line will echo other curves, regardless of size. Negative and positive shapes are very idea-provoking. You sawed out a single shape from each metal piece, but you could have made disconnected shapes as part of a single pattern, and cut each out separately, leaving some silver to frame each part of the design. Try another pair of earrings with the design made this way. A long narrow pair—1½″ x ½″ works well—but you can make them larger if you like. When you make a disconnected pattern, you must put the positive shapes in your scrap box for future use. Perhaps you would like to try to combine curved lines and angles this time. Work your design on paper first, very carefully, so that the small parts of the pattern harmonize with each other to make a harmonious whole. Remember to reverse your pattern, for the left and right earrings.

The piercing technique illustrated in Plate 10 makes very effective designs and is an excellent way to practice on the jeweler's saw. Be sure to plan your design carefully so none of the sections are competely sawed out.

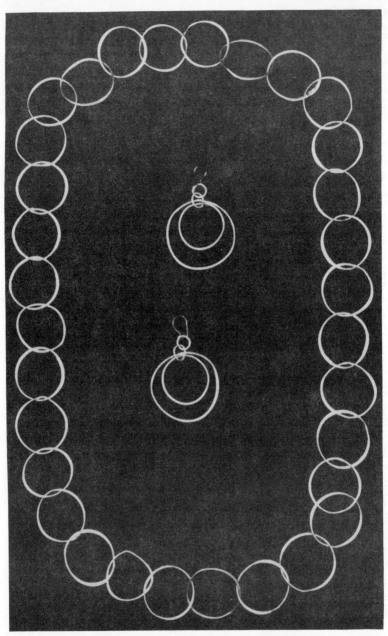

Plate 11: One of the many ways to join silver hoops.

simple soldering

Ring

MATERIALS:
2½- to 3-inch piece 16 gauge half-round wire
 (measure ring size)

TOOLS:
Torch (#20)
Jeweler's saw and No. 1 blade
 (#17 and #18)
Asbestos square (#21)
Charcoal block (#24)
Flux and brush (#25 & 19)
Iron binding wire (#26)
Soldering tweezers (#16)
Scriber-poker (#14)
Hard silver solder (#29)
Plate shear (#5)
Half-round needle file (#10)
Flat needle file (#10)
Pickle solution (#27)

Clean water in shallow bowl
Mallet (and dowel stick or
 piece of pipe or ring
 mandrel) (#7)
Round-nosed pliers (#3)
Copper tongs or old wooden
 spoon
Steel wool wad, No. 0/4
 (#31)
Medium emery cloth (#30)
Crocus cloth (#32)
Rouge cloth (#33)
Saw frame and No. 1 blade
 (#17 and 18)

Numbers refer to tools as identified and discussed in Chapter 3.

STEP 1: This project is completely basic and simple: you will make a circular band without decoration. Make all your preparations first. Cut snippets of solder with the shear. Cut more than you need and store in a small medicine bottle or flat metal box, marked so you know which grade of solder it is. Make your pickling solution and fill a small pot or bowl with clean water. Set your charcoal block on the asbestos square, and have your poker, soldering tweezers, and jar of flux with a clean, small-tipped brush handy. Measure your ring size with a narrow strip of paper, fastened with scotch tape. Be sure it will slide over the knuckle of your finger, but do not make it too loose.

STEP 2: Use scriber to mark on silver wire where the paper measure ends. Thread saw frame with No. 1 blade (teeth face down and out) and saw off the required length for your ring size.

STEP 3: With round-nosed pliers, working first at one end of wire, then at other before you bend the center portion, make an oval shape, flattened where the two ends meet. They must meet exactly if the soldering is to be effective, so hold the ends together and examine against the light to be sure that there are no gaps. Use the flat needle file to true the ends. Keep checking, so you don't file away too much silver. If you slide the flat file between the ends of the ring and hold the ends against both sides of the file (not too tightly, or the file will stick) you can do both ends at the same time and make them match more easily.

STEP 4: Apply tension to the two ends. This means that you keep the circlet in the same shape and push the ends past each other, then out again, until the metal gets enough spring to hold in place when the ends are mated (see Fig. 83). Be

Fig. 83

104

sure they fit together exactly. If you find tension difficult to get, wrap iron binding wire across the ring half-way down from the open seam, and twist tightly to hold the ends together during the soldering process (see Fig. 84).

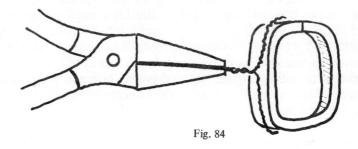

Fig. 84

STEP 5: Flux entire circlet, inside and out, and set on the asbestos square with the open seam down. Use the charcoal block as a back wall to balance the ring against. Use the point of the flux brush to set two snippets of hard solder in place across the inner seam line, touching both sides of the seam at once (see Fig. 85).

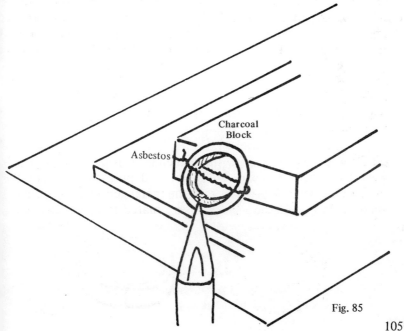

Charcoal Block

Asbestos

Fig. 85

STEP 6: Light the torch and dry the flux with a small soft flame (yellowed at the end and rounded in shape). Keep the flame moving. The flux will bubble and if the solder snippets jump out of place, push them back with the point of the poker. Don't hold the flame too close to the silver and keep it moving in a circle around the entire ring.

STEP 7: Increase the heat until you have a small blue cone of light inside a longer cone of light. The greatest heat is at the point of the inner cone. Move the flame, starting at one side of the seam, around the circle to the opposite side of the seam and back again, moving the flame slowly but steadily. You must always heat the heaviest metal (in this case, the ring band) before you heat the seam and the solder. The flux will turn brownish, then contract and peel as it liquifies; the silver will first get shining white, then get a rosy glow. At this point, move the flame in a continuous circular motion instead of back and forth, heating the seam and the solder too. You will see the solder "flash" as it melts, and it will be brighter than the silver ring as it flows into the joint. Remove the heat at once. Turn off the torch. Use the soldering tweezers to drop the ring *after* you remove the binding wire if you used it) into the pickling solution. *Do not touch the liquid with the tweezers.* If you contaminate the pickle your silver ring will come out wearing a hard-to-remove copper coat.

STEP 8: When the ring looks white remove it to clean water, using either the copper tongs, an old wooden spoon, or even your fingers. The pickle solution is not dangerous as is acid, and you'll be rinsing your hand at once, anyway, when you put the ring in clean water. Dry it and check the soldering by trying to open the seam to the side. It should not open. If it does open, you were probably afraid of the torch and removed the heat before the solder flowed. In that case, reclose, reflux and resolder.

STEP 9: Use the flat side of the half-round needle file to work diagonally across the outside part of the seam, with light strokes. Lift for the return stroke, for the file cuts only on the stroke *away* from you. Don't file on the seam or you will cut a groove. Use the round side of the file on the inner part of the seam, moving the file in a sweeping motion, ahead and to the side, following the curve of the ring.

STEP 10: Use a small wad of steel wool to rub piece clean, inside and out. Set on your mandrel and tap it lightly with the mallet to make it a true circle (see Fig. 86). Try it for size. If you have made it too large, you will either have to wear it on another finger or saw it open to resize it. If it is too small, you can stretch it a little, by tapping it gently with the flat face of the metal hammer. Keep trying it for size so you don't stretch it too much.

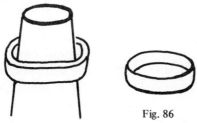

Fig. 86

STEP 11: Polish with small pieces of medium emery paper doubled over the inside and outside, so you can rub up both sides with one motion. Repeat with the crocus cloth. Use rouge cloth for a final high shine.

Variations on the Theme:
Double Hoop Earrings

MATERIALS:
One 18-inch piece 18 gauge round wire
One pair ear wires, or screw-backs with ring attached

TOOLS:
Same as for Ring, plus medium and easy solders
Ochre powder and brush

Two sizes of dowel sticks (1-inch and ¾-inch instead of ring mandrel)

STEP 1: Each earring consists of four rings—one large, one medium and two very small—linked but free hanging. Procedure is same as for Ring. Coil wire into shape to fit on charcoal block, and tie with iron binding wire. Brush thin layer of flux over entire coil. Light torch and anneal with soft flame, moving flame continuously around circle so wire does not burn until flux dries, burns off and silver glows rosy red. Turn off torch, and drop into pickle (first removing binding wire). Then into clean water. Dry, and straighten with fingers.

STEP 2: Make all eight rings. Wind twice around larger dowel stick, and saw through to make two rings. Repeat for two more rings on second dowel stick. Make four individual rings on round-nosed pliers, using part of nose above the center, so rings won't be too small, or wrap four rings around a No. 5 knitting needle. Use flat needle file to make ends of all rings flat for tight fit and snap together with tension. Check against light to be sure the fit is tight.

STEP 3: Use medium solder snippets (one for each ring) to solder together the ends of each of the four larger rings and two of the small ones. Flux and solder each ring separately.

STEPS 4-8: Repeat Steps 4-8 of Ring. After pickling and rinsing, file gently across seam line on each ring to make it disappear. Then paint spot with ochre paste (to make ochre paste: mix ¼ teaspoon ochre powder with a few drops of water).

STEP 9: Use last small ring to connect one ring of each size (three in all), snap closed and solder with easy solder. When solder flows, rinse ochre off with hot water, pickle, and rinse. Check seam and file clean. The last ring you soldered will be the center ring of the earring. From it the two larger rings will hang down and the other small ring will suspend it after it has been threaded into the little open ring of the screwback, or hung on the ear wire.

STEP 10: Polish with pieces of emery and crocus cloth.

Shoulder Bag Hook

MATERIALS:
One 5" x ¼" piece 16 gauge flat rectangular wire
One 3-piece safety catch pin back

TOOLS:

The same as for Ring	Ochre powder
Hard and easy solder	Brush

For anyone who uses a shoulder bag, this hook is an attractive and convenient piece of jewelry. It can be left plain, or textured by hammering or nail-patterned as in Chapter 7. It is worn pinned to the shoulder, hook end up; and keeps the strap of the shoulder-bag from sliding off.

STEP 1: Thread saw with No. 1 blade (teeth facing down and out) and cut flat wire in two pieces—one 2-inch and one 3-inch.

STEP 2: Use the flat side of the half-round file to round corners on both pieces, and bevel the edges all around both.

STEP 3 (Optional): Using stamps and hammer as in Chapter 7, texture about 1¼" at one end of the longer piece, and about ¾" on each end of the shorter one. You can use the round head of the ball-pein hammer to make dents if you don't want a "set" pattern. Turn pieces over and use mallet to flatten out any bends in the wire.

STEP 4: Fit the two pieces together in a T-shape (see Fig. 87). The textured ends of the short piece should face up. This piece is on bottom. The longer piece fits on top, with the textured end as bottom of the T, and texturing underneath. This will show when the hook is formed later. Bind together in X-shape with iron binding wire, and set on charcoal block (see Fig. 87). Flux whole piece. Cut six snippets of hard solder and lay 3 on each side of the T-stem, touching both stem and cross-bar on bottom (see Fig. 88).

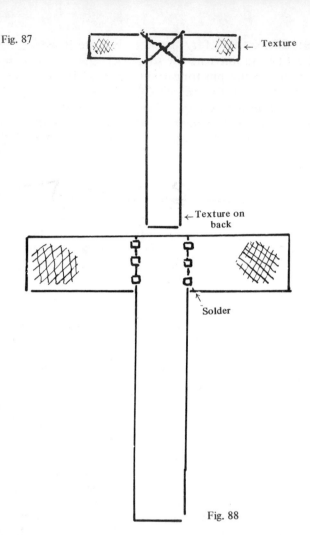

Fig. 87

Texture ←

← Texture on
back

Solder

Fig. 88

STEPS 5-7: Repeat Steps 5-7 of Ring. Remove binding wire, pickle, rinse, dry and check soldering. Paint both sides of stem with ochre paste.

STEP 8: Lay face down on charcoal block and line up the safety catch part and the joint end of the pin along the cross-bar of the T. Measure the distance carefully, using the pin tong, so you don't put them too far apart. Make a small X with the scriber where each part will sit.

STEP 9: Check the safety catch to be sure it works. Set it with the little rabbit ears on top, with the opening throat facing down, so the pin tong will hold in when you fasten it. On the bottom of the catch and of the joint end, there should be either a tiny cup or a little flat spot. Holding the piece (one at a time) in the tweezers, flux and melt a snippet of easy solder on this bottom (see Fig. 89). Pickle. Flux

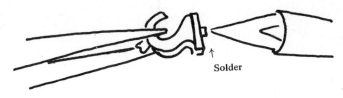

Solder

Fig. 89

cross-bar and melt a snippet of easy solder on top of each X spot (see Fig. 90). Do safety catch first, holding it in the tweezers, just over the X spot, while you remelt the solder there. Don't use too much heat or you'll fuse the rabbit ears and the catch won't open. As the solder on the cross-bar melts, set the catch down on it, *in the right position,* and play the flame on it once more to make sure that the solder grabs. Stand for a few moments to cool, then line up the joint end sighting along cross-bar to be sure the position is

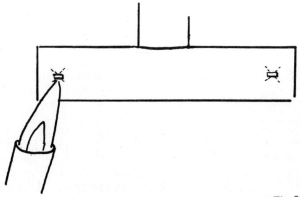

Fig. 90

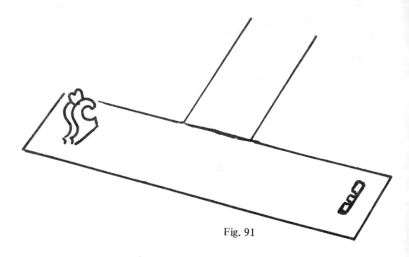

Fig. 91

correct. Be sure that the two ears of the joint end line up with the top and bottom lines of the cross-bar, then remelt the solder on the second X and set the little joint down in place (see Fig. 91). You must work quickly (and very surely) to set the parts in place while the solder is still molten. Cool a little, then use the tweezers to work the rabbit ears back and forth. If you have fused them, you must remelt the solder and substitute another safety catch. Pickle, rinse and dry.

STEP 10: Set the pin tong into the joint end, with the wires in the holes in the joint and use the flat nosed pliers to push the two flaps together, making the tong secure.

STEP 11: Rub the entire piece briskly with a wad of steel wool, and use the medium emery cloth to polish and clean. Use either a piece of the cloth or the buff, whichever you are more comfortable with. Go over it with the crocus cloth, to clean completely.

STEP 12: Use the round-nosed pliers to turn the end of the T-stem up into a hook. The textured portion will now face up, as the top curve of the hook (see Fig. 92). See that the part attached to the cross-bar lies flat. Rub with rouge cloth for a high shine.

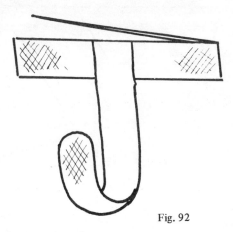

Fig. 92

Design Interlude

The projects for this exercise in basic soldering have required little thought about design. But you will do more and more soldering as you make other pieces of jewelry, and for most of those, the soldering technique will be only a means of executing the design. The choice between formal and informal design is really a matter of taste. No one can (or should) make the decision for you. Neither form of design is better as long as both include balance and proportion.

On the one hand, the very essence of formal design often makes it easier for a novice, because once half a good pattern is made, it is simple to create the other half by duplication. But again, the very looseness of informal design often allows for more variety of line, and a more personal feeling in the finished piece. It's your work, and it's up to you, no one else.

Just remember, in all your designs, the area you do not fill is as much a part of your pattern as the spaces you do fill. Try to see each piece as a whole, in the setting for which it was designed. The hand wearing the ring becomes part of it, as does the air inside the moving hoops of the gypsy earrings, and the ear from which it hangs. The pattern remains an isolated thing only while it is flat on paper. The moment you execute it in the third dimension is the moment it takes on a life of its own. A piece should always look as if it were part of the person wearing it.

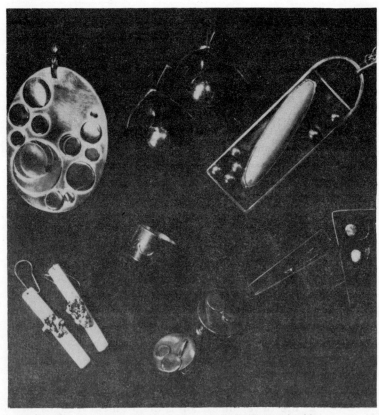

Plate 12: Sweat-soldering: the band ring is silver and gold;
the disc pendant silver and copper.

sweat-soldering

Belt Buckle

MATERIALS:
One 2½" x 3½" piece 16 gauge silver
One 15-inch piece 14 gauge half-round wire
One 4-inch piece 18 gauge round wire
One 2½-inch piece ¼ x 18 gauge flat wire
One 1½-inch piece 14 gauge round wire
Leather or suede strip, five inches longer than waist and
  1½" wide
Two metal grommets

TOOLS:
Torch (#20)
Asbestos square (#21)
Wire mesh square (#22)
Charcoal block (#24)
Flux and brush (#25 & 19)
Ochre powder and brush
  (#28 and 19)
Iron binding wire (#26)
Solder tweezers (#16)
Scriber-poker (#14)
Hard, medium and easy silver
  solder (#29)
Round-nosed pliers (#3)
Flat-nosed pliers (#4)
Nail and hammer (#6)

Hand-drill and No. 54 bit
  (#13)
Saw frame and No. 1 blade
  (#17 and 18)
Half-round file (#9)
Half-round needle file (#10)
Knitting needles No. 2 (or
  No. 3) and No. 5
Medium emery cloth (#30)
Crocus cloth (#31)
Steel wool, No. 2/0 (#32)
Rouge cloth (#33)
Paper
Soft pencil
Rubber cement

Numbers refer to tools as identified and discussed in Chapter 3.

STEP 1: Outline your silver blank on paper. Draw line down the center and draw half a simple geometric design. Darken the lines with soft pencil, fold on center line and transfer pattern by rubbing the back of the paper. Glue paper to silver blank with rubber cement and set aside to dry completely.

STEP 2: Measure your wires against the parts of your pattern and cut the wires to size with the saw. In Fig. 93 the eight lines marked "A" (border) were cut from 14 gauge half-round wire. The six pieces marked "B" were cut from 18 gauge round wire. The four small jump rings marked "C" were wrapped on a No. 3 knitting needle, but they could have been turned individually with the round-nosed pliers. The large center ring marked "D" was made on a No. 5 knitting needle, but could have been made on the heaviest part of the round-nosed pliers, too. Use the half-round needle file to smooth and round all the ends of all the straight wire pieces.

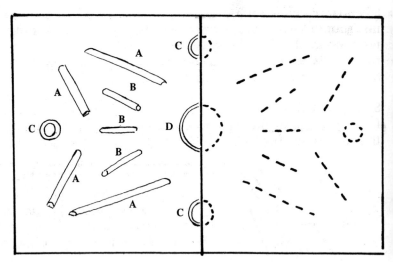

Fig. 93

STEP 3: File both ends of all the rings to make each close tightly together. Use tension to snap each ring closed. That is, move the ends of each ring past each other on the same circular line, then gently pull apart and fit together. They

116

should make a tiny snapping sound and hold in place without binding. Set one ring on the charcoal, set on the asbestos square, and flux with brush. Set a snippet of hard solder under the open seam of the ring, touching both sides of the open seam. Light the torch and use a soft flame (not sharply pointed and with yellow end) to dry the flux.

STEP 4: Increase the flame just a little, so there is less yellow and a more-pointed cone. *Keep the flame moving* around the edge of the ring. The flux will bubble, turn brownish, then golden as it peels off and the silver will get a rosy glow. Lift the torch, pulling the flame up, but without removing it from the piece. At this point your snippet of solder should flash and flow up toward the flame (solder always flows toward the heat) to fill the joint. Turn off the torch. Drop the ring into pickle solution—just the ring, *not* the tweezers. Rinse. Dry. Check soldering. Lay aside and repeat until all the rings are soldered.

STEP 5: Use the scriber to mark the pattern lines on the metal through the paper. Soak paper off silver and go over the lines to be sure they are clear. Use the half-round file to round all corners and bevel the edges all around the blank. Smooth with needle file if it feels rough to your finger.

STEP 6: With flat-nosed pliers, make a right-angle bend ½″ from each end of the flat wire (see Fig. 94). Check the fit of this little bridge against the back of the buckle blank, and file

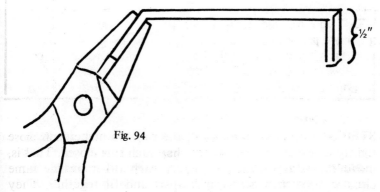

Fig. 94

117

flat with flat side of half-round file to make a tight joint. Check against the light to make sure there are no gaps. Repeat Step 4 to solder the bridge with hard solder across the 2½″ measure about 1″ in from the edge and centered (see Fig. 95). If the ends of the bridge fit well, you should not need to tie it in place with the binding wire. Paint both soldered joints with ochre paste (mix ½ teaspoon of ochre powder with a few drops water), using brush.

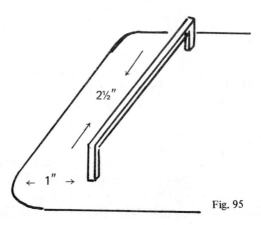

Fig. 95

STEP 7: About an inch in from the other end of the blank, find the center spot and use nail as center punch, with hammer to make a small dent. Fit the No. 54 drill bit into the chuck of the hand drill and bore a hole through the blank. One of the rings, soldered on the face of the blank, will hide this.

STEP 8: Use the half-round file (and the needle file to finish) to round one end of the 14 gauge round wire, tapering it slightly for about ½″. Fit the other end into the hole (the back of the blank should face up). If it does not balance upright in the hole, wrap a piece of iron binding wire around it, make a sharp angled bend and push the end of the wire into the charcoal block to hold it erect during soldering (see Fig. 96). Flux and use two snippets of hard solder (one on each side of the upright silver wire lying on the base touching the upright. Dry with soft flame, increase heat and concentrate heat *on the base,* moving the flame slowly around the

118

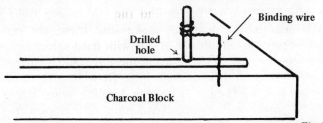

Binding wire

Drilled
hole

Charcoal Block

Fig. 96

bottom of the wire while the flux melts. Keep the flame away from the other end of the buckle, but the end where you are working should glow before you turn the heat on the upright. The solder will melt and flow into the hole in the base. Turn off torch and remove binding wire. Wash off ochre with hot water before you place piece in pickle solution. Rinse and check the soldering. Repaint both joints of brush and the base of the upright with ochre. Use the flat-nosed pliers to bend the top of the round wire in toward the center of the buckle, until it is the same height as the bridge at the other end (see Fig. 97). This way the buckle will balance when you turn it over to work on the front.

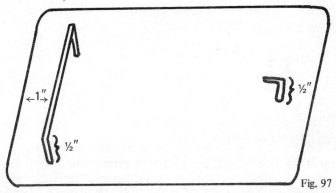

←1″→

½″

½″

Fig. 97

STEP 9: Make sure that all the pieces of half-round wire are completely flat and fit properly on the face of the buckle on your pattern lines. Set all the pieces, flat side up, on the charcoal block and flux. Place snippets of easy solder at ¼-inch intervals on the flat side, using point of flux brush. Dry with soft flame, then increase heat just a little and keep flame moving up and down length of each bit of wire until

119

the solder melts over the entire piece. Drop in pickle solution and repeat process with the bits of round wire and with each ring. Rinse and dry all pieces.

STEP 10: Reflux each piece and set in position on the pattern. Flux entire face of buckle and dry with soft flame. Use poker to push back into place any bits that move when the flux bubbles and dries. Increase heat and keep flame moving on the base around the wire design until you see the flux peel off and the solder remelt. Remove the flame at once and stand for a moment or two to cool a little. Try the strips with the tweezers to check the soldering. Then pickle, rinse and dry.

What you have just done is sweat-soldering. It will not work unless all the parts are flat and fit tightly together. You can use the poker to press the parts down as the solder starts to remelt, but it will probably not be necessary.

STEP 11: You can give the entire buckle a bright finish by rubbing with the steel wool pad, then with the emery cloth and crocus buffs before you use the rouge cloth. You may, however, emphasize your pattern by antiquing the background (see Chapter 7, Bracelet directions).

STEP 12: To assemble your belt, thread one end of the leather strip under the bridge and around it and rivet together with two Dritz grommets and the hammer. Make a series of spaced holes in center of other end, and fasten the belt by catching the round wire hook through a hole for a comfortable fit (see Fig. 98).

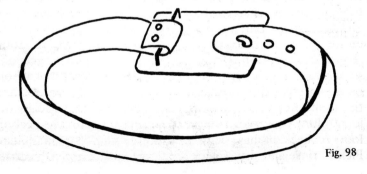

Fig. 98

Variations on the Theme:
Pendant with Mixed Metal Design

MATERIALS:
One 2½" x 1½" oval, round, square or free-form shape in
  18 gauge silver
Assortment of bits of scrap metal, silver, copper, brass
One 1½-inch piece 16 gauge round wire
Chain for hanging pendant

TOOLS:
Same as for Belt Buckle

STEP 1: If you want to cut your own shape instead of purchasing it, use saw and blade No. 1. Incise the shape on a silver blank with the scriber and saw as close to the outside of the line as you can. File with half-round file true to shape and bevel the edges.

STEP 2: Use the round-nosed pliers to make an oval-shaped loop with the small piece of round wire. Squeeze the ends flat against each other, but do not make a continuous oval. File the ends smooth and rounded with the needle file.

STEP 3: Slide the top of your shape between the loose ends of the loop, making sure it is centered on the top of the shape and squeeze together again. Check to make sure that it makes a tight joint, and if necessary, file a tiny flat spot on the inside of each bottom end of the loop. It should not need binding. Set on charcoal block, with loop end off the block and large shape flat, so there is no problem of balance. Flux entire piece and place two snippets of hard solder on either side of base of loop. Dry with soft flame, replacing bubbling solder bits with poker. Increase flame and heat the whole base, moving flame constantly, before you heat the loop and the joint. Keep heat moving until solder melts and fills the joint. Turn over with tweezers and repeat, soldering back of loop to back of base with two snippets of medium solder. Pickle, rinse and dry. Check soldering and paint with ochre.

STEP 4: Plan your pattern and repeat Step 9 of the Belt Buckle with all the pieces of your pattern.

STEP 5: Reflux pieces and set in position on face of your piece, now lying on the charcoal block (again with hanger-loop off edge for balance), set on asbestos square. Flux entire piece and dry with soft flame. Increase heat to small blue cone and heat entire piece, moving flame around the pattern parts to heat the base first. When base heats and glows a little bit, throw flame on each pattern piece in turn, using poker to hold it flat as the solder underneath remelts and runs out to the edges. This should happen quickly because the easy solder has a low melting point. Move from one piece to another until all the parts of your pattern are fixed in place. Turn off the torch. Pickle, rinse and dry.

STEP 6: Repeat Step 11 of Belt Buckle to polish (and antique, if you wish). Hang on a commercial chain.

Cuff Links

MATERIALS:
Two 1-inch discs, ovals or squares of 18 gauge silver
Small bits of scrap metal (silver, brass, copper)
One pair cuff link backs with stainless steel springs

TOOLS:
Same as for Belt Buckle plus Tweezers (#15)

Number refers to tool as identified and discussed in Chapter 3.

STEP 1: Plan your design. Keep it simple, remembering that your background piece of metal is quite small. Remember also that, as for earrings, you will need a right and a left cuff link mirroring each other.

STEP 2: Repeat Step 9 of Belt Buckle, using *hard* solder snippets melted on the back of your pattern parts. Paint whole face with ochre after pickling and rinsing.

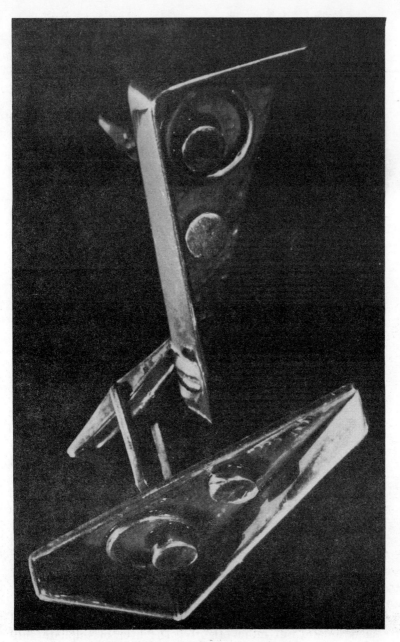

Plate 13: Cuff links with antiqued background.

123

STEP 3: Lay the two pieces design side down on opposite ends of charcoal block and solder cuff link backs on, one at a time. Flux entire back, after marking center dot with scriber. Hold finding in tweezers, flux base and melt on a snippet or two of easy solder. Pickle and rinse, then reflux.

STEP 4: Set in position on marked spot and dry flux with soft flame. Increase heat and move flame around bottom of the finding *on* the base, using the tweezers to hold the piece in position until base heats and solder remelts and runs out to edges. Repeat with second link.

STEP 5: Wash ochre off with hot water. Rub with steel wool on both sides.

STEP 6: Antique if you wish and polish, repeating Step 22 of Belt Buckle.

Design Interlude

Sweat-soldering of flat surfaces can be a fine technique for building up three-dimensional designs. It is not necessary to solder and resolder with graduated grades of solder, because all the parts can have the solder flowed on the backs, and then, when they are set in place, either next to or on top of each other, the heat of the torch will remelt all the solder at the same time, for a simple operation. However, all the parts must be flat or they will not make proper joins. This method is especially good for modern, geometric patterns. Make a relationship between the design you choose for the separate parts and the shape of the base on which they will lie, so that your entire piece is one design, rather than a design laid on a background.

This kind of design introduces color as an additional element, as well as shape. The buckle used antiquing to darken the color of the background silver and make the polished shapes stand out more brightly. The liver of sulphate antiquing is effective only when the piece has high and low spots, and gives detail much more importance than polishing can do by itself. You will not want to use it all the time, but it can be very handsome in the right place. The pendant added copper color to the color of the silver. You might investigate brass added to the silver, without or with copper. You might also try shapes of Nu-Gold, a brass alloy with a lovely true-gold color. Pile the pieces on each other; place them touching or separated in formal balance or in off-center design. Move the pieces around on the silver background before you plan your pattern on paper, so that you will learn to visualize the effects of the contrasting metal colors. Silver with copper looks warmer than silver with silver. Nu-Gold (because real gold is too expensive to use) adds great richness to a design, even when used in very small quantities. Like colors in a painting, the color metal casts on tangent metal pieces makes shadows that are very appealing to the eye.

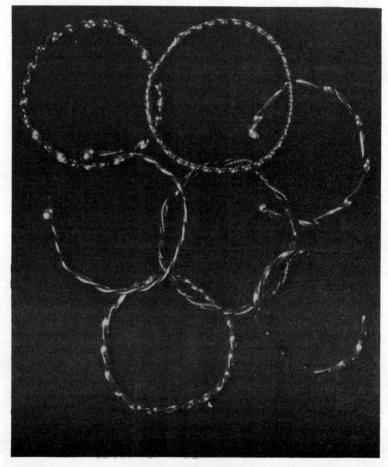

Plate 14: Assorted bangles.

twisted wire

Twisted wires of other metals (copper, brass or gold) make very effective bangles that are always popular. They can be left open or soldered to close. The open bracelet should be about six inches long; the closed bangle measures 8¼" for the average hand, allowing for room to slip over the widest part of the hand. Measure your own fist across the knuckles for an accurate measure. The 24-inch piece of wire allows for waste. There are several methods of twisting the wire, which we will explore.

Bangle Made with Two Vises

MATERIALS:
One 24-inch piece 14 gauge round wire

TOOLS:

Bench vise (#12)
Hand vise (#11)
Torch (#20)
Asbestos square (#21)
Pickling solution (#27)
Charcoal block (#24)
Magnesium block (#00)
Flux (#25)
Flux brush (#19)
Hard silver solder, easy
  grade (#29)

Flat file (#8)
Iron binding wire (#26)
Mallet (#7) and bracelet
  mandrel (rolling pin or
  baseball bat will also do)
Steel wool No. 2 (#32)
Fine emery cloth (#30)
Crocus cloth (#31)
Rouge cloth (#33)
Saw frame and No. 1 blades
  (#17 & 18)

Numbers refer to tools as identified and discussed in Chapter 3.

STEP 1: Wrap the wire in a coil, secure with binding wire and anneal it quickly, using the soft flame on the torch. Remember to keep the flame moving so you don't burn the wire. Quench in cold water. Dry.

STEP 2: Fold the wire in two and insert the loose ends, as close together as possible, about ½-inch into the jaws of the bench vise. Close tightly so the ends will not pull loose. Insert the folded end into the hand vise and close the wing-nut tightly. Pull wire taut, straightening it with one hand, as you use your other hand to pull with the hand vise.

STEP 3: Turn the hand vise either to the left or the right (it doesn't matter with round wire) and keep turning it until you have made a tight rope of the two wires (see Fig. 99). Loosen both ends from the vises and measure the length—you should have approximately 8¼".

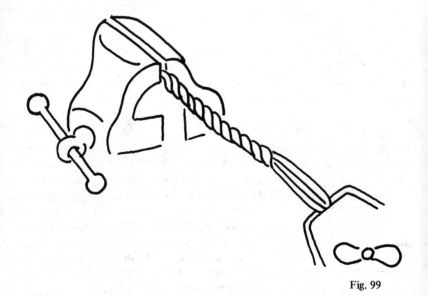

Fig. 99

STEP 4: Thread your saw frame and cut between *(not across)* loops at both ends so that the ends will fit together neatly for soldering (see Fig. 100). Save your scraps.

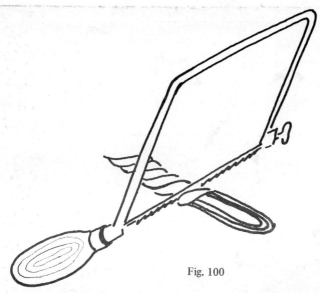

Fig. 100

STEP 5: File the ends smooth with the flat file. An easy way to make sure that the faces of both ends meet closely (remember that solder will not fill a gap) is to form an oval shape, lining up the two ends of the twist. Insert your file between the ends, with both ends touching the faces of the file (see Fig. 101). You will be smoothing both ends of the

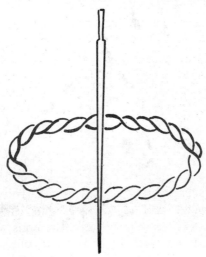

Fig. 101

twisted wire at the same time this way. Check from time to time to see if more filing is needed—holding the ends together, hold the piece up to the light.

STEP 6: Leave the piece in the oval shape for soldering. Tie with binding wire with the open seam in the center. Flux the entire twist and set on the asbestos square with the open seam at the bottom. Balance the piece against the charcoal block. (If you find it too difficult to balance the circlet on end, make two staples of the binding wire and secure the circlet to the magnesium block with these, using the charcoal block as backing for additional security.)

STEP 7: Cut snippets of easy grade hard silver solder and lay them across the seam (three or four pieces should be enough). Use the tip of the flux brush to lay them in place.

STEP 8: Light the torch and use a soft flame to dry the flux, using the poker to push back stray snippings. Increase the heat to a pointed cone and heat the entire piece. Keep your flame moving around the circle, starting at the joint and moving around the piece to the other side of the joint and then back again. Don't move the flame too rapidly. Pickle, rinse and dry. (If the solder balls up or refuses to flow, the piece is not clean, or you have withdrawn the heat too soon. If this happens clean the piece, removing the binding wire first, in the pickle and start again.)

STEP 9: Place soldered piece on mandrel and use the mallet to mold it into a round shape. Take care not to mark or flatten the twist.

STEP 10: With the needle file make light strokes *across* the seam (remember that the file cuts only on the stroke *away* from you) until the seam is no longer visible. Don't press down too hard or you will file a depression where the seam was. You should be able to turn the bangle without seeing where the seam line was.

STEP 11: Polish with emery cloth and steel wool pad, and finish with crocus cloth and rouge cloth, as in previous projects.

Variations on the Theme: Bangle with Round and Half-round Wires

MATERIALS:
One 12-inch piece 10 gauge half-round wire
One 24-inch piece 10 gauge half-round wire

TOOLS:
Same as for first Bangle, plus   Medium grade hard silver
Hand-drill (#13)   solder
Cup-hook

Number refers to tools as identified and discussed in Chapter 3.

The same combination of materials will give you two different wire twists, depending on whether you use the rounded side of the half-round wire or the flat side. Both are handsome.

STEP 1: Anneal both pieces of wire, with the soft flame of the torch and quench in cold water. Dry. Set the half-round wire aside.

STEP 2: Fold the 18 gauge round wire in half and insert the loose ends into the bench vise, close together. Tighten well. Slip the open end of the cup-hook (fastened into the chuck of the hand-drill) through the loop made by the closed bend (see Fig. 102). Pull the wire taut and straighten with fingers if necessary. Turn the handle of the hand-drill rapidly to make a tight rope of the doubled round wire. Look carefully to make sure that it is twisting evenly. Loosen the bench vise to remove the ends and remove from the cup-hook.

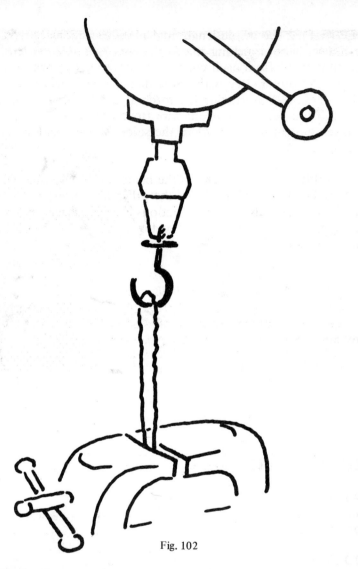

Fig. 102

STEP 3: Straighten the half-round wire with the mallet if necessary. Bind the twisted wire to the flat side of the half-round wire with the iron binding wire. Set on the charcoal block on the asbestos pad and use the magnesium block as an extension for the needed length. Cut six snippets of medium solder.

STEP 4: Flux the whole length and place the solder bits on the heavier wire—touching the smaller twist of wire at both ends (about ½″ from each end)—and at several points down through the center. Dry with a soft flame, increase the flame and solder together, moving the torch at all times and being sure that you heat the bottom wire first, since that is larger. Remove the binding wire when the solder flows. Pickle and rinse. Dry.

STEP 5: Place ½″ of one end in the bench vise. Close tightly. Tighten the hand vise on ½″ of the other end. Twist to the right until you have ½-inch sections of round wire with twisted wire lying between the sections. Loosen both vises and remove the twist.

STEPS 6-14: Measure 8¼″ when you remove the twist and repeat Steps 4-11 of the first Bangle.

Note: A completely different twist results from soldering the twisted round wire on the curved side of the half-round wire. The materials and methods are exactly the same.

Square Wire Bangle

MATERIALS:
One 10-piece 10 gauge square wire (use 8 gauge or 6 gauge for heavier bangles)

TOOLS:
Same as for first Bangle

STEP 1: Repeat Step 1 of first Bangle.

STEP 2: Attach ends of wire in both bench vise and hand

vise and twist slowly to the right, making the twist as tight or as loose as you like. (A tight twist will result in a shorter length, so you may need an additional inch of wire.)

STEPS 3-10: Repeat Steps 4-11 of first Bangle.

Flat Wire Bangle

MATERIALS:
One 10-inch piece 6 x 18 gauge flat wire

TOOLS:
Same as for first Bangle

STEPS 1-10: Repeat steps 1-10 of Square Wire Bangle.

Design Interlude

Rings can often be made from the left-over ends of brace lets. If not, a 2½-inch length of 16 gauge square wire can be twisted and the untwisted ends filed and soldered together Earrings are made the same as bracelets except you use thinner wires. Twenty-four inches of 20 gauge round wire will give you two huge gypsy earrings plus a ring. Twelve inches of 20 gauge flat wire will give you a pair of twisted earrings of more ordinary size. For earrings you'll need small 20 gauge jump rings (see Chapter 12).

Other design possibilities with twisted wire are endless You might find it useful to keep a notebook of different twists. Count the number of turns you make for a tight twist and for various looser ones. Keep your notes accurate, so you can reproduce a twist at will. Combine round wires twisted to the right, with half-round, flat or square wires twisted to the left. You can make a herringbone effect by soldering together two lengths of twisted round wires, one set twisted to the right and one set twisted to the left. You can combine silver wire with copper wire or with brass wire, or with both. Combine twisted wires with flat wires (lay the twists along both sides of the flat and solder together) for a bracelet with rope edges. Maybe a wide bracelet of different twists would appeal to you. Leave it open, by filing the ends round before you shape it. Experiment with others and have fun.

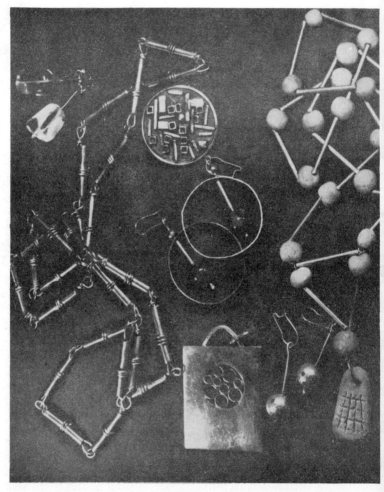

Plate 15: Beads and tubing add infinite variety of shape and color.

136

CHAPTER 12

tubing & beads

Silver beads are hollow and ideal for stringing. Tubing is useful to separate hanging parts of an earring or necklace, and to keep them in a desired position. Each must be used so that it becomes an integral part of the design.

The tubing comes in many sizes, both round and square. Beads of silver and semi-precious stones can be purchased in sizes from 3 mm. to 10 mm. They also come drilled with only one hole for mounting on pegs for rings, pins and pendants.

Earrings

MATERIALS:
One 2-inch piece tubing 1/8" in diameter
One 6-inch piece 20 gauge round wire
One 7-inch piece 8 x 22 gauge flat wire
Two ½-inch beads (if using silver or semi-precious stone get 10 mm)
Two ¼-inch beads (5 mm in silver or semi-precious stones)
One pair earwires (or screw-backs) with hanging ring.

TOOLS:

Jeweler's saw and blades
 No. 1/0 (#17 & 18)
Torch (#20)
Asbestos square (#21)
Charcoal block (#24)
Flux and brush (#25 & 19)
Ochre paste and brush
 (#28 and 19)
Hard silver solder, medium
 and easy (#29)
Plate shear (#5)
Poker (#14)
Soldering tweezers (#16)

Half-round file (#9)
Needle files, half-round and
 round (#10)
Hand-drill and No. 52 bit
 (#13)
Nail and hammer (#6)
Round-nosed pliers (#3)
Dowel or piping about ¾"
 in diameter
Steel wool No. 2/0 (#32)
Medium emery cloth (#30)
Crocus cloth (#31)
Rouge cloth (#33)

Numbers refer to tools as identified and discussed in Chapter 3.

STEP 1: Anneal the piece of flat wire with a soft flame. Quench. Dry.

STEP 2: Measure, then saw in half across the center.

STEP 3: Using the nail (as center punch) and hammer, make dent on center spot of each piece of flat wire. Drill holes through with hand-drill.

STEP 4: Form wire into circle, using mallet and dowel stick or pipe. File ends to match (check against the light to be sure the joint is tight). You can use "tension" to hold the two ends together, by pushing the ends past each other (still in circle shape) and then pulling them apart and fitting them together. Do this a few times until the joint sits securely together without binding wire. Set on asbestos square with open joint down, flux whole piece, set two or three snippets of medium solder across joint and dry with soft flame. Increase the flame and solder, heating the whole ring in circular motion starting on one side of joint and working around to the other side. Remove heat as soon as the solder flows. Pickle, rinse and dry. Set aside.

STEP 5: Cut round wire in half. Coat each small length of wire with yellow ochre paste (see Page 47) up to ½″ from one end. Let dry. Hold the coated end of one piece with soldering tweezers, and flux the clean ½″ at top. Light the torch and increase it to a blue-coned flame. Play this cone on the fluxed end of the wire until the flux dries and the metal "balls." It will melt and contract almost with one motion—the ochre prevents it from balling further. Repeat with the other piece of wire. Rinse with hot water to remove ochre. Place in pickle and rinse to clean. Set aside.

STEP 6: Thread the saw frame with No. 1/0 blade (teeth down and out) and slice the tubing into four pieces—two pieces 3/16″ long, and two 5/16″ long. Measure carefully and mark with the scriber so they match. Try to saw directly *on* the line. Rub the ends on the flat side of the file to smooth and straighten the ends.

STEP 7: Use steel wool and a piece of fine emery cloth to polish both sides of each piece you have made.

STEP 8: On a piece of the round wire thread one large bead. The balled end will keep it on the wire. Add a 5/16-inch length of tubing, then thread the end of the wire *up* through the hole in the circlet of flat wire. Add the 3/16-inch length of tubing and the small bead. Make a ring, using the round-nosed pliers on the other end of the wire. Close the ring tightly, and make sure that it sits in the same direction as the loop hangs, not at angles to it (see Fig. 103). Use the pliers to

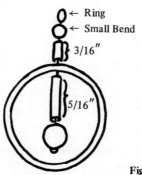

Fig. 103

turn the ring to the proper position, if necessary. If you are using silver beads, you can flux the ring and solder it with a bit of easy solder. If you are using ceramic beads or beads of stone, do not try to solder or you may ruin the beads. Repeat with other earring.

STEP 9: Use the rouge cloth to polish all the silver parts, being careful not to spoil the shape of your hoop.

STEP 10: Assemble by hanging on ear-wires. (If you used screw-backs, open the little ring to the side, *not outwards,* hang the ring on top of the piece on it, close the ring tightly with your pliers.)

Variations on the Theme: Round Tubing Pendant

MATERIALS:
One 6-inch piece 10 x 16 gauge flat wire or 10-gauge half-round wire;

Four inches round wire tubing in assorted diameters (1/8'', 3/16'', ¼'');
Commercial silver chain

TOOLS:
Same as for earrings, plus
Hard solder

STEP 1: File the ends of the flat wire smooth, fit together tightly and solder into a continuous band, using hard solder. Pickle, rinse, and dry. Using your fingers and round-nosed pliers, make a shape to frame the pendant. It need not be completely regular—I used a teardrop as shown in Plate 16. With the pliers bend the pointed end to the left so it forms an angle to the rest of the shape. (This is going to be the "ring" through which the chain is threaded for hanging.)

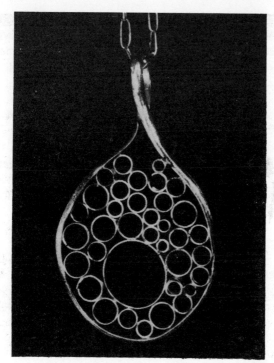

Plate 16: Pendant of tubing slices can be
worn with either face front.

STEP 2: On a piece of paper trace the inner shape of the
piece. Set the paper on a small stiff backing (cardboard or
wood).

STEP 3: Thread your saw with No. 1/0 blade and slice the
various pieces of tubing into pieces—any size from 3/16″ to
5/16″. Smooth the ends on the flat side of the file. Arrange
them on the paper pattern to be sure they fill the space. Each
ring should touch at least two others as you work in towards
the center. The most central rings should touch three others.
The entire assemblage should touch the outer shape at all
points. Leave the area at the top clear of rings.

STEP 4: Lay your charcoal block on top of the design and
lift up the base on which you have set your paper pattern.
Hold together with both hands and turn upside down.

Remove the base and paper pattern and replace any rings that have moved out of place. Be sure you have filled the area completely—check by setting wire frame gently in position so as not to disturb the assemblage. Make any necessary adjustments and remove frame.

STEP 5: Gently flux the whole assemblage. Set aside to dry while you cut snippets of medium solder—cut a lot. When the flux is completely dry, use the tip of the flux brush to place one tiny piece of solder at each spot where one ring touches another. Make sure that every connecting spot is covered. Dry with a soft flame. Don't hold the flame too close to the piece or you will blow away the solder bits.

STEP 6: Increase the flame slightly and move the flame slowly over the whole piece until the solder flows. Keep the torch moving so that you do not melt any of the rings. Remove the heat as soon as the solder flows. Pickle, rinse and check to make sure that all the rings are soldered together at all points. If any loose points turn up, paint all the soldered joints with ochre, flux the loose parts, and resolder with medium solder.

STEP 7: Set the soldered rings on the charcoal block and fit the outer shape to it. You may have to change the shape slightly if any of the rings moved in the soldering.

STEP 8: Paint the rings with ochre paste (see Page 47), but stay away from the outer edge where you want the solder to connect it to the frame. Paint the seam of the frame too. (If you have positioned the seam up at the top of the piece it will be even safer). Flux the outer edges of the ring pattern and the frame (except where the ochre is). Dry with a soft flame.

STEP 9: With the tip of your flux brush set snippets of easy solder every ½″ around the edges of your piece, connecting the frame and the outer rings. Dry with soft flame. Increase heat and move torch slowly around the outside of the rim, moving inside only occasionally, until the entire piece heats and the solder flows. Remove the heat at once. Rinse in hot water to remove ochre. Pickle, rinse clean and check the soldering.

STEP 10: With needle file, file gently across the top seam until seam line disappears.

STEP 11: Polish with No. 4 steel wool on outside frame. Then use fine emery cloth and crocus cloth. Rub very gently over the tops of the circles with the steel wool. Then gently rub the whole thing with rouge cloth. Hang on the chain.

Design Interlude

When working with silver beads and tubing, the materials themselves limit the size and shape of your design—since the beads are rarely cut smaller than 3 mm or larger than 10 mm, and tubing is limited to round or square shape. You have, however, opened another door if you use stone beads—the doorway to color. Beads can be purchased in almost any color under the sun from the black of jet or obsidian to the milky white of pearls. You can combine beads of different sizes and different colors. You can find hand-made ceramic or porcelain beads with colors already combined, and there are marvelous African glass beads formed in odd shapes with exotic color combinations and patterns. The important thing to remember is over-all size. The encircling metal shape must not be so large that the hanging beads are lost, or so small that they are crowded. Remember that even if the tubing pieces are soldered together in a unit, these are essentially *hanging* pieces of jewelry, with a sense of open space. You should therefore balance the piece, with the heaviest concentration of design at the bottom. Doodle some patterns on paper. Combine round tubing slices with round, oval and square outer shapes. Try combining round and square tubing within the frame. You might make square earring frames and use square tubing with your beads. You'll find each variation different and interesting.

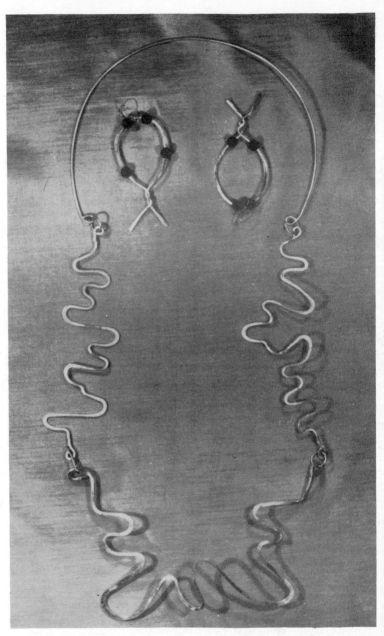

Plate 17: Areas of forging are clear in this necklace and earring set.

144

forging

Cold forging is the method by which silver and gold (and other nonferrous metals) are worked with hammers on steel stakes or anvils. During the process the shape of the metal is changed because the metal is pushed in front of the hammer as it is thinned out. The shaping, therefore, is always in the direction of the hammer blows, so you must make them even, and aim the hammer to land where you want it to, not at random. You are going to do very elementary forging on a flat anvil. There are shaped stakes available for more intricate designs but they are expensive and not really best for beginners. Use the piece of scrap copper wire to practice on before using the silver. Use light even blows to flatten the wire at one end. Then aim your blows, working from the center out, to broaden the metal into either a round or oval shape. Decide which shape you want, so you will know whether you have succeeded with the forging. You can widen other areas on the wire, too. They can be on the same side of the wire or at right angles to each other. Be careful not to make the metal too thin. You will feel the metal respond to your blows. When it begins to feel stiff and unmoving, anneal it to make it soft and workable again.

Open Bracelet

MATERIALS:
One 9-inch piece 10 gauge square wire;
Piece of scrap copper wire.

TOOLS:

Torch (#20)
Asbestos square (#21)
Charcoal block (#24)
Flux and brush (#25 & 19)
Hammer (#6)
Anvil (or metal block or
  old iron)
Bench vise (to support iron)
  (#12)
Mallet (#7)

Round-nosed pliers (#3)
Half-round file (#9)
Half-round needle file (#10)
Bracelet mandrel (or rolling
  pin, pipe or baseball bat)
Pickling solution (#27)
Dish of clean water
Fine steel wool (#31)
Crocus cloth (#32)
Rouge cloth (#33)

Numbers refer to tools as identified and discussed in Chapter 3.

STEP 1: Anneal the wire. *Note:* 10 gauge wire takes longer to heat up than the 18 and 20 gauge wire you're accustomed to. Use the medium tip of the torch for a larger flame and keep the flame moving so you do not burn the wire. Remove flame when it glows reddish. Pickle rinse, dry and straighten.

STEP 2: The design is extremely simple—the flattened ends (oval-shaped) will lie next to each other when the bracelet is formed, and since it is open, it is adjustable for size (see Fig. 104).

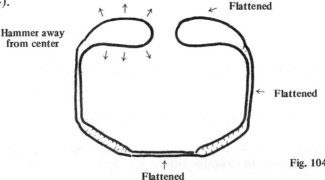

Hammer away
from center

Flattened

Flattened

Flattened

Fig. 104

146

STEP 3: Lay one end of the wire on the anvil, and hold the length of the wire in one hand, to keep it steady as you work. Be careful to hit the wire only with the flat face of the hammer, not with the edges, or you will nick the wire. Start about 1¼" from the end, using light, even blows, to work toward the end. Keep the blows even and close to each other—the metal will dent badly if the blows are uneven or too heavy. Work from your forearm, not from the shoulder. When the wire is flattened (but not too thin) you will find that it has also lengthened a little. Now aim your blows from the center out to the edges, first on one side, then the other, until you have widened the wire into an oval shape. If the wire feels stiff, anneal it again. When you are pleased with your shape, repeat it at the other end of the wire. Anneal when necessary, because if you do not, the metal will begin to strain and may crack.

STEP 4: Use the file to smooth and round all edges where you have worked the metal. Go over it again with the needle file until it feels smooth.

STEP 5: Use the mallet, which will not mark the wire, and a bracelet mandrel to shape the wire into a curve to fit your wrist.

STEP 6: Rub the bracelet, front and back, with fine steel wool, then with a piece of doubled-over crocus cloth so you can polish all sides of the wire at once. (Use the rouge cloth for a high shine.

Variation on the Theme: Hairpin

MATERIALS:
One 12-inch piece 12 gauge round wire

TOOLS:
Same as for Open Bracelet, minus mandrel

STEP 1: Anneal wire, and straighten it again. The hair pin is made to wear "Geisha Girl Fashion" in a knot of long hair.

STEP 2: Use the round-nosed pliers and your fingers to make a free-form curved design with 5″ of the wire. Do not cross the wires over each other in the design, or the hammer may break them. Keep the curves open and uncomplicated, balanced but not regular (see Fig. 105 for suggestion).

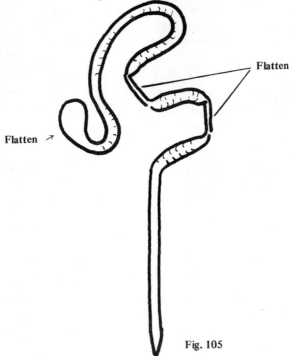

Flatten

Flatten

Fig. 105

STEP 3: Decide which portions of the design are to be flattened and made wider. You can flatten the entire head, but the contrast between round and flat curves is prettier. Lay the head on the anvil, and aim the blows so that you flatten only the areas you wish to flatten. Keep the blows light and even, and do not nick the wire with the edge of the hammer face. Work from side to side across the wire in the areas you are forging. When you are satisfied with your design, turn the head over and hammer the entire back *very* lightly to stiffen the metal and help hold its shape.

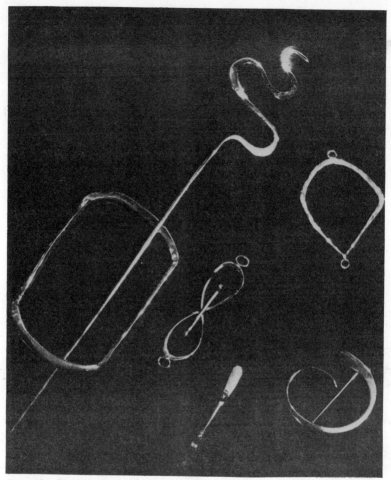

Plate 18: Forging: the head of the hairpin is completely flattened and the ends are forged in opposite directions.

STEP 4: Use the flat side of the file to taper the bottom two inches of the other end, turning the piece as you work to taper it evenly. Round the point by going over the tapered end with the needle file until it is smooth to the touch.

STEP 5: Polish with the steel wool and the crocus cloth. Use rouge cloth for a high shine.

149

Earrings with Beads

MATERIALS:
One 12-inch piece 18 gauge round wire
Eight small beads (4 mm.-4.5 mm.)
One pair ear wires.

TOOLS:
Same as for Open Bracelet, minus mandrel

STEP 1: Anneal the wire. Straighten and cut in half.

STEP 2: Use your fingers and the round-nosed pliers to make a circle or oval shape of one piece of wire. Start the curve in the center of the wire and use about 3½″ of wire. String on four beads, then twist the wire together twice, to hold the shape, and spread the ends apart slightly.

STEP 3: Push two beads to the top of the circlet and two to the bottom, one on either side of the twist. Set the side of the circlet on the anvil, being careful that the beads are over the edge. Hammer the side lightly to flatten it, then reverse and flatten the other side (see Fig. 106). The ends can be placed on the edge of the anvil at the same time and flattened. Repeat with second earring.

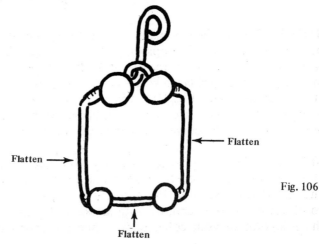

Flatten

Flatten

Flatten

Fig. 106

150

STEP 4: Use the needle file to smooth the edges where you have worked the metal. Round the tips or file them square.

STEP 5: Polish with fine steel wool, a scrap of doubled crocus cloth, and the rouge cloth. Hang on the ear wires between the two beads at the top. The flattened areas will prevent the beads from sliding out of place.

Necklace

MATERIALS:
One 14-inch piece 16 gauge round wire (for back)
One 24-inch piece 16 gauge square wire (for sides)
One 18-inch piece 14 gauge square wire (for center)
One 5-inch piece 18 gauge round wire (for jump rings)
    (optional).

TOOLS:
Same as for Open Bracelet,   Ochre and brush (#28 & 19)
    plus   And minus the mandrel
No. 5 knitting needle
Hard & easy silver solder (#29)

Numbers refer to tools as identified and discussed in Chapter 3.

STEP 1: The necklace is made in four pieces. The pieces can be connected with self-loops or with jump rings. The jumps will not be as organic to the design, but they will add mobility to the necklace. With paper and pencil, lay out a curved design (see Fig. 107 for a suggestion). The small X-marks show where the parts connect to each other. Mark where you want the curves flattened and broadened.

STEP 2: Make coils of each wire and anneal each one separately. Pickle. Remove 16 gauge round wire coil, rinse, dry and straighten. Use your fingers to curve the wire to conform comfortably to the curve of your neck. It should extend to the midpoint of your collar bone, when the ends have been

151

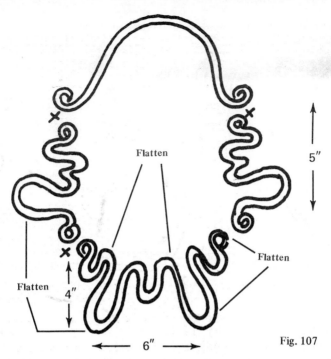

Flatten

Flatten

Flatten

Flatten

5"

4"

6"

Fig. 107

formed into loops. There is an allowance for waste. Allow about ¾" for the loop, if you must cut the wire. The loops should be formed on the heaviest part of the round-nosed pliers, and should face out, away from the center curve. Make the loops a tight fit with the wire. Set aside.

STEP 3: Rinse and dry the 16 gauge square wire. Straighten and cut in half. Use your fingers and the round-nosed pliers to make a series of open curves, with loops on both ends, so that you end with a 5-inch pattern. Repeat with second side wire. Be sure that you have made your patterns in mirror image, for left and right sides. The designs need not be identical, but should be similar in feeling. Decide, before you make the pattern for the left side, whether or not you will use jump rings as connectors. If you are not, make a loop only at the top of the pattern, leave 1" of the bottom straight, and use it to make a catch (see Fig. 108). If you are using jump rings, make the bottom loop, but leave it loose, because you will not solder it closed. Set aside.

152

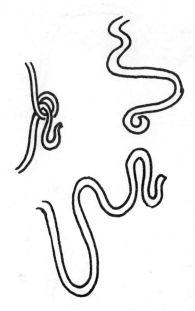

Fig. 108

STEP 4: Rinse and dry 14 gauge square wire. Straighten. Form loops at both ends, then make a pattern with larger curves for the center part of your necklace. The finished pattern should measure approximately six inches across, and be three to four inches deep.

STEP 5: If you are using jump rings, rinse and dry the 18 gauge round wire and wrap on the No. 5 knitting needle to make four jump rings. Cut or saw to separate. File ends to mate and set aside. Make catch (see Fig. 62).

STEP 6: If you are using jump rings as connectors, mate the ends of all loops (except on the bottom of the left side design piece) to the adjoining wire, filing if necessary for a tight fit. Solder each loop closed with hard solder snippets. If you are *not* using jump rings, solder *only* the loops of the back center sections.

STEP 7: Lay the center section on the anvil, holding it flat with one hand, and forge parts of each curve to flatten and broaden them. Keep the blows light and even as you work,

153

and do not nick the wire with the edge of the hammer face. Aim your blows and move the section from time to time, so that you work from the inner edge of the wire toward the outer edge. Do not make the wire too thin. When you have finished, turn the piece over and hammer *very* lightly across the whole back to flatten the design and stiffen it a little. Repeat with the two side pieces. Hammer very lightly on the piece that fits around your neck—you want to strengthen the curve, not flatten it.

STEP 8: Paint all the soldered joints with ochre paste (see page 47). Dry. If you are using jump rings, connect each loop of the back section to the top loop of one of the side sections. Be sure you use the proper side piece (left or right) at this time, so the necklace will hang well. Connect the bottom loop of the right side section to the loop at the right side of the center section with the third jump ring. Hang the fourth jump ring on the loop at the left side of the center section. Use the unsoldered loop at the bottom of the left side section to slide on the small loop of the catch and close the loop tightly. Solder, one at a time, each jump ring, using easy solder snippets. Solder the last loop closed with easy solder. Pickle.

If you are not using jump rings to connect the parts, use the pliers to turn the already soldered loops of the center and back pieces at right angles to the body of the piece. Open the loops on the top of the side sections (being sure they face in the proper directions) and thread on the loops of the back section. Close the loops tightly. Open the loop at the bottom of the right side section and connect to the right hand loop of the center section. Close tightly and solder all loops closed with easy solder. Wash off the ochre with hot water before you pickle. Rinse dry and check soldering.

STEP 9: Rub each part of the necklace with fine steel wool, then with doubled piece of crocus cloth. Use both hands to curve the two side sections and the center section to conform with the curve of your body. You will need to make a very shallow curve only. Try the necklace on to be sure the curve is right. Use the rouge cloth for a final high shine.

Design Interlude

One of the problems you run into with all jewelry pieces is that of making the piece "sit right" or "hang right." Just as a pin mechanism should be placed above center so that the fabric to which the pin is fastened is not pulled or torn and the design on the face invisible, so earrings must be balanced to hang so that the ear is comfortable and the design shows up to the best advantage.

This often becomes a matter of personal tolerance. The outsize gypsy hoop is unendurable to many women. Once a piece of jewelry is in place, you should be able to forget it. If you find earrings tangling with your hair, resting on your shoulders or dragging at your earlobes, the design is obviously not for you.

A necklace, too, should be comfortable to wear. The largest elements of the design should always lie toward the center. Witness the constant popularity of the graduated bead necklace. The largest element of the design is usually what draws the eye, too, so you do not want it to sit on your stomach. Neither should it bounce when you move, or jut out into space. This is true, especially, of the forged necklace. Ideally, all the elements of the design should become one with the wearer, conforming in shape so that it is a true body ornament, rather than an extraneous piece that looks as if it were an afterthought.

Plate 19: Bezels made for round, oval, square and free-form shapes.

CHAPTER 14

bezeled
stones

A bezel is a thin metal frame that holds a stone in place. Its basic function is security, not decoration, although it can be given added decorative accents. This frame is usually made of bezel wire, a flat 24 or 26 gauge wire, ready-made wide (¼") or narrow (1/8"), in fine and sterling silver. Narrow bezel wire is used except when the stone has a high dome. Fine silver is preferred because it has a higher melting point than sterling, but is more malleable and easier to push into place without endangering the stone. The bezel should be exactly fitted to the stone; it is always better to make it a shade smaller rather than larger. If you make it too large, you will have to cut, resize and resolder. If you make it too small, it can be stretched by light hammering. Inside the bezel there must be a small shelf to seat the stone, and this must be precisely fitted as well. Oval and round shapes are easiest to make, but even stones of irregular shape can be bezeled. Until you are more experienced, stick to the hard stones: agates, quartzes and jaspers. It would be a pity to design a mount for a beautiful stone only to have that stone break in two in the mounting.

Ring

MATERIALS:

One 2½- to 3-inch piece (depending on ring size) 16 gauge half-round wire

One cabochon cut agate or quartz stone

One circle or oval 18 gauge silver piece 1/16″ larger in diameter than stone

One 2- to 3-inch piece 18 or 20 gauge round wire

One 3-inch piece fine silver narrow bezel wire.

TOOLS:

Saw frame and No. 1 blade (#17 and 18)	Ochre and brush (#28 & 19)
Plate shear (#5)	Pickling solution (#27)
Round-nosed pliers (#3)	Dish of clean water
Flat-nosed pliers (#4)	Soldering tweezers (#16)
Mallet (#7)	Iron binding wire (#26)
Ring mandrel	Poker (#14)
Flat file (#8)	Hard, medium and easy silver solder (#29)
Needle files, flat and half-round (#10)	Medium and fine emery cloth (#30)
Torch (#20)	Crocus cloth (#31)
Asbestos square (#21)	Rouge cloth (#33)
Magnesium block (#23)	Burnisher or stone setter
Charcoal block (#24)	
Flux and brush (#25 & 19)	

Numbers refer to tools as identified and discussed in Chapter 3.

STEP 1: Anneal bezel wire. Be careful—it is fragile.

STEP 2: Lay the stone flat on the work table and wrap the bezel wire around it. Rest the bezel wire flat to the table too, to be sure you are measuring at the base of the stone. Mark with scriber where the overlap starts and cut away waste with shear (see Fig. 109). Make the cut straight so you will have less filing to do. True the ends, using flat needle file, then fit them together with tension.

STEP 3: Set ring on charcoal block, seam side down, balanc-

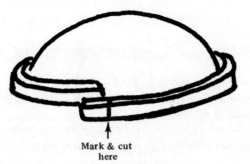

Fig. 109

**Mark & cut
here**

ing it against the magnesium block. Flux entire piece, set two snippets of hard solder across the seam, and dry with soft flame, replacing bubbling solder bits with the poker. Increase flame to small blue cone and keep flame moving back and forth around the ring, from one side of the seam around to the other and then back again, until the flux burns off and the metal has heated. Then move the flame full circle over the seam until the solder flashes and runs to fill the joint. Don't get the point of the flame too close to the wire or you will melt the bezel. Pickle, rinse and dry. Check soldering. Test stone for fit.

STEP 4: Lay flat file on piece of clean paper on table top, and rub the edges of the bezel ring in a circular motion on the file, to straighten the edge. Turn over and repeat. (This is always necessary if you have cut your own bezel from a sheet, but purchased wire will need very little truing.) File across seam, with needle files, inside and out, until they vanish. Set aside.

STEP 5: Anneal the half-round wire. Use the *angle* of the 3-square needle file to make a shallow groove ¼″ from each end of the wire. The groove is on the flat side of the wire, and will make it easier for you to make a sharp bend in the wire at that point. Use the flat-nosed pliers to make this ¼″ bend at right angles, the bends at both ends of the wire to face in the same direction. File the round side of the wire on these end pieces to flatten a little and taper them thinner. Test these flat spots against the disc to which it will be soldered, for a tight fit. Your fingers should be enough to

159

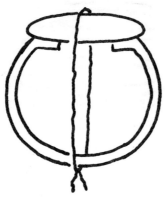

Fig. 110

bend the wire to form a ring shank—the ends need not fit together if you need the extra space. When the flattened tops meet the disc exactly (*center* the disc, please), bind the two pieces together with the binding wire (see Fig. 110).

STEP 6: Flux the entire unit and set, shank up, on the charcoal block. Dry flux with soft flame, and set snippets of hard solder on the base and touching each side of the ring shank ends. You will need at least four bits of solder. Move the torch, with the flame increased to a small cone, around the base then up and around the shank continuously until the pieces heat evenly, when the solder will flash and run in to fill the joints. Turn off torch, remove binding wire. Pickle, rinse, dry and check soldering.

STEP 7: Use the flat needle file to smooth the tapered part of the angled ends of the shank, so you will not feel them when you try on the ring. Paint the joints with ochre paste.

STEP 8: Make sure that the bezel ring makes a tight joint with the face of the disc. Center it, and flux lightly (the drying flux acts like glue). Balance it, shank down, between the charcoal and magnesium blocks. Make a circlet of the scrap wire to fit inside the bezel. It should match the bezel, touching all around. (This is essential if you are mounting a transparent stone and cutting out the center of the back-plate; it is less important in a solid mount, but it *is* a good habit to form.) With inner ring in position, use binding wire

160

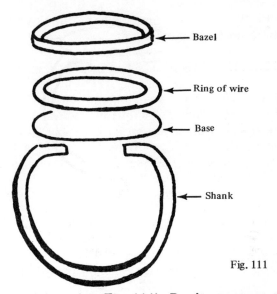

Bazel

Ring of wire

Base

Shank

Fig. 111

to attach bezel and base (see Fig. 111). Don't use so much wire that you have no room to place your solder bits. Flux entire top. Set snippets of easy solder ¼" apart, around the inner curve of the bezel, touching bezel, base and inner ring at one time. You may find it easier to set the bits of solder in place touching base and bezel *before* you lay in the inner ring and bind the piece. In that case, set the solder bits when you center the bezel and dry them into position with the bezel. (Once you are more experienced you will use the side of the poker, laid across the bezel ring to hold the pieces flat.) You can also solder the inner ring into position with medium solder before the bezel is mated to the base. This is a good practice if more than one stone is to be mounted on the same base, or if the bezel is to get a decorative frame of twisted or beaded wire. Increase the flame to a small cone and keep it moving around the outer curve of the bezel, pointing at the base. For every three circles you make around the bezel, move the flame into the center to heat the base there. When the solder starts to flash, move the flame around several more times outside and in, to be sure that all the solder bits melt and grab. You should have soldered all three parts together at one time. Cut away binding wire. Wash ochre off with hot water. Pickle, rinse, dry and check soldering.

161

STEP 9: Rub with fine steel wool then with pieces of fine emery cloth and crocus cloth.

STEP 10: Set the ring shank into the jaws of the bench vise, protected with pieces of scrap leather or heavy fabric. Tighten enough to hold, but not enough to crush the wire. Fit the stone into the bezel, and hold it firmly in place with one finger while you use the burnisher to push the bezel in and up over the edge of the stone (just a little) to hold it securely in place (see Fig. 112). Work one side of the stone, then the opposite side, before you work around in a circular motion. The burnisher will not scratch the bezel, and will polish the metal as it pushes it into place. When the stone is set, rub with the rouge cloth for a high shine.

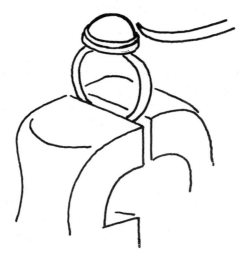

Fig. 112

Variations on the Theme: Indian Bolo Slide

MATERIALS:
One 2½-inch square 18 gauge silver plate
One 3-inch piece 20 gauge round or square scrap wire
One 3-inch piece fine silver bezel wire
One oval cabochon stone (not more than one inch long)
Bolo slide finding, cord and tips.

TOOLS:
Same as for Ring, plus
Hammer (#6)
Objects for stamping

Paper and soft pencil
Rubber cement

Number refers to tool as identified and discussed in Chapter 3.

STEP 1: Outline the silver blank on paper, draw line down through the center. Since the bolo slide, as jewelry, originated in the Southwest, an Indian pattern is appropriate for it. This is also the time to combine several of the techniques you have already used: sawing and stamping. Execute half of an American Indian pattern: Thunderbird, tepee, sun, warbonnet, etc. Fold on center line and rub back to transfer lines for a complete pattern. Sharpen lines. Trace around the stone in the center. Glue to blank with rubber cement and dry completely.

STEP 2: Use scriber to scratch through the paper pattern the central line of the stone and the pattern lines to be stamped. Thread the saw frame with the No. 1 blade (teeth facing down and out) and saw out the pattern, staying *just* outside the line. Wash off paper and dry silver. Go over pattern lines where necessary.

STEP 3: Use needle files to smooth and bevel all edges. Then use the hammer and your "stamps," as you did in Chapter 7, to mark all your design lines. Don't strike the stamp so hard that you cut through the metal. When the design is finished, turn over, and use the mallet lightly to flatten the base again. Set aside.

STEPS 4-7: Repeat Steps 1-4 of the Ring to make the bezel. Check the stone for fit. With the stone in place, check against the space in the center of your base and draw a new outline with the scriber if needed.

STEP 8: Turn blank, face down, on charcoal block and solder the bolo slide finding, using hard solder, centered in the width, and a little above the center line midpoint. Paint the joint with ochre after pickling.

STEP 9: Form inner bezel from scrap wire. Repeat Step 8 of the Ring and solder bezel to the face of the slide, using easy solder.

STEP 10: Rub with fine steel wool, then with fine emery cloth and crocus cloth to clean and polish.

STEP 11 (optional): If you would give added definition to your pattern lines, use liver of sulphate solution and a clean brush to paint only the lines. Use cleanser on a wet finger tip to clean off excess darkness.

STEP 12: Repeat Step 10 of Ring to set your stone. Rub front and back with rouge cloth, and assemble by sliding cord through the finding loops before you attach and close the metal tips on the ends of the cord.

Cuff Links with Square Stones

MATERIALS:
Two small square stones, cabochon or table cut, about
  ½-inch square
Two ¾" x 1" 18 gauge silver oblongs (cut or buy)
One 5-inch piece fine silver narrow bezel wire
One pair cufflink findings.

TOOLS:
Same as for Ring

STEPS 1-4: Repeat Steps 1-4 of Ring, making a bezel joint *away* from a corner (see Fig. 113). Try stone for fit.

STEP 5: With stone in place, so shape does not distort, mark with scriber a small area at each corner to be cut away. Do not mark all the way to the bottom; you must leave a little metal to solder to the base (see Fig. 114). With stone still in

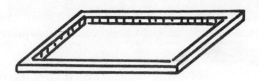

Fig. 113

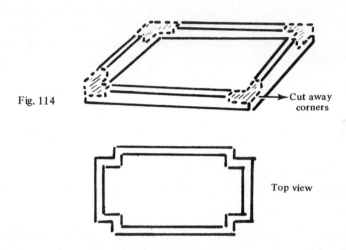

Fig. 114

Cut away corners

Top view

place, outline bezel on blank, centered or off-side. If you are setting the stone off-side, remember that the other link will have to be off-centered to the opposite side. Remove stone and set aside.

STEP 6: Texture the areas around the bezel site, using either stamps or the ball head of the hammer. Keep the blows light and even. Reverse blank and flatten with mallet.

STEP 7: Repeat Step 8 of the Ring with medium solder—this bezel does not require an inner ring.

STEP 8: Thread saw frame with fine blade and *very* carefully saw away the marked metal area at each corner of the bezel. Don't remove too much silver. Smooth the edges of the cuts with the 3-square needle file. True shape with flat-nosed pliers. Paint entire face with ochre.

165

STEP 9: Set face down on charcoal block. Center link finding and mark spot with scriber. (Remember findings are also for left and right links, and use the correct one.) Flux entire back of the blank and base of finding (hold in soldering tweezers) and melt on a snippet of easy solder. Reflux. Increase flame and heat base, holding the finding above the base, so that the heat will reach it as well. Keep the flame moving. When the flux begins to remelt, set the finding down carefully on the marked spot and hold it in place while you circle the flame around it several times more. Turn off torch. Disengage the tweezers. Pickle, rinse and dry.

STEP 10: Rub front and back with fine steel wool, then with fine emery cloth and crocus cloth pieces to polish. Shine up with rouge cloth.

Fig. 115

STEP 11: Start working, with stone in place, on one side of the bezel. Use burnisher to push the side in and up over the top of the stone (see Fig. 115). Hold the stone down with one hand while you work. Move to the opposite side and repeat. Then do the third and fourth sides. The corners of the stone will show, but the framing strips will secure it. *Repeat for second cuff link,* remembering to make it a mirror image of the completed one.

166

Design Interlude

Any stone or object of smooth even shape can be bezeled, but the easiest bezel to make will be round or oval. It is better to stick to prongs or a wrapping, if there are projections or rough irregularities. Again, the harder stones present less danger of damage to the stone itself.

Transparent and translucent stones are usually made with the center of the base sawed away behind the stone, after the bezel is fitted and soldered into place. Opaque stones, unless they are so heavy that the mount must be lightened the same way, are made with solid backs. See the Reference Lists to find the colors and hardness of the more popular stones. Some of the least expensive stones come in the loveliest colors and markings.

When the bezel is made for a curved surface (a formed ring without a top plate, or a bracelet) the base of the bezel must be filed to conform to the curve on which it will sit. When you have more experience you will be able to solder several bezels to the same base.

In addition to bezeling stones, you might consider cameos, antique buttons or medals, round or oval shells (fragile, so take care), square or round ancient coins or seals, scarabs, carved coral heads, baroque pearls, or onyx tiki.

Plate 20: The "turtle" is the simplest form of prong mounting.

pronged mounts

Pendant

MATERIALS:
One 3" x 1½" piece 18 gauge silver (approximate)
One stone (or other object) at least 1" in diameter
One silver chain.

TOOLS:
Rubber Cement
Saw frame & No. 1 blade
  (#17 & 18)
Half-round file (#9)
Half-round needle file
  (#10)
Round-nosed pliers (#4)
Nail and hammer (#6)
Hand-drill and No. 54 bit
  (#13)

Torch (#20)
Asbestos square (# 21)
Charcoal block (#24)
Flux and brush (#25 & 19)
Easy silver solder (#29)
Pickling solution (#27)
Medium steel wool (#31)
Medium emery cloth (#30)
Crocus cloth (#32)
Rouge cloth (#33)

Numbers refer to tools as identified and discussed in Chapter 3.

STEP 1: This "turtle" pendant is one of simplest of pronged designs, popular with primitive artists for centuries. On paper, make a careful outline of the stone or object to be mounted. Draw a matching shape ¼" inside the outline. This will be the ledge on which your object sits. Draw a frame around the shape, allowing ¾" (measure carefully) from the top of the shape to the top line of the frame, ½" from the outline to each side, and ¼" at the bottom. Measure the dimensions of the frame to see how much silver plate you will need. Draw the head and 4 legs each ¼" wide (see Fig. 116). Cut out the shape and glue to silver with rubber cement. Dry completely.

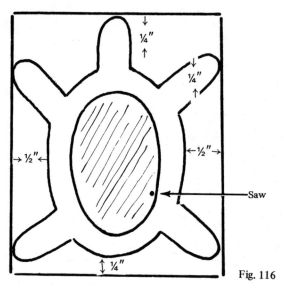

Fig. 116

STEP 2: Use the nail as a center punch and hammer a mark just inside the inner line. Use the hand drill with No. 54 bit to bore a hole. (This step may be omitted if you are mounting any object with a flat back, but cutting out the center will make the pendant lighter to wear.) Fasten blade into top of the saw frame, thread through the hole (be sure that the paper pattern faces *up*), tighten into the bottom of the saw frame and saw out the inner shape as close to the line as possible, but do not saw directly on the line. Loosen blade to remove silver.

170

STEP 3: Retighten blade in saw frame and saw out the outer shape. Don't push; let the saw do the work, and remember to move the silver not the saw, especially going around corners.

STEP 4: Use half-round file to smooth all the edges. Use the round side on the inner cut and the flat side on the outside. Round the ends of the legs. Make sure the top of the head is straight. Repeat with half-round needle file until all edges are smooth.

STEP 5: With the round-nosed pliers bend the head back and down into as large a loop as it will form. Close the end tightly against the back of the frame (see Fig. 117). Flux entire piece and solder closed with 2 or 3 snippets of easy solder. Pickle, rinse, dry and check soldering.

Fig. 117

STEP 6: Rub front and back with steel wool, then with emery buff and crocus buff, to clean and polish silver.

STEP 7: Set your stone in position. It should sit easily on the ¼" frame. With the round-nosed pliers bend each leg up over the stone, holding the stone in place with your thumb as you work. Close each leg as close to the stone as you can. (If you have a burnisher use it to push the prongs in and down.) Shine with rouge cloth and hang on the chain.

171

Variations on the Theme:
Circle-in-the-square—A Pin-Pendant

MATERIALS:
One 2-inch square piece 18 gauge silver
One 9-inch piece 18 gauge round wire
One ¾-inch piece silver tubing, 1/8" diameter
Cabochon stone or specimen, 1-inch diameter
Three-piece pin back with safety catch
One 1¼-inch piece silver scrap wire.

TOOLS:
Same as for Pendant, plus   Wire mesh square
Anvil   Medium solder
Scriber

STEP 1: Trace the outline of the stone on the silver with a pencil. Then with the scriber mark a line just inside this pencil outline. (The center hole must be a little smaller than the stone is, or it will fall through instead of sitting in place on the mount.) Use the hammer and nail to mark a dent inside the scribed line. Bore hole with hand drill and No. 56 bit. Thread saw blade through hole (scribed line must face up), tighten into saw frame and cut out center of blank inside and close to scribed line.

STEP 2: Use half-round file's round side to true edges of inner cut and bevel them slightly from top only (see Fig. 118). Be careful not to file away too much material. Test with stone from time to time to be sure it still has an edge to sit on. Round outer corners slightly and smooth all outer edges. Finish with half-round needle file so edges are completely smooth.

STEP 3: Set stone in place and decide where you want it held by the prongs. The round silver wire called for allows six 1½-inch prongs, but you may want five or even seven. Try not to obscure the markings in the stone with the prongs.

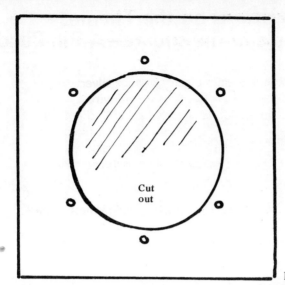

Fig. 118

Mark with pencil the position of each prong, touching the edge of the stone. Remove stone and set aside. Use nail and hammer to dent each spot. Bore holes with hand drill and No. 56 bit.

STEP 4: Cut round wire into equal length prongs. Lay one end of each prong on anvil (or metal plate) and flatten ¼″ of the end with light blows from the hammer. Don't make the wire too thin; flatten it just a little. Then round off top with needle file and smooth the edges, on all the prongs. Try with the stone for size, by setting the prongs in place in the holes and setting stone in center. If you are mounting an irregular shape you may need prongs of varying lengths or longer or shorter prongs. To find an exact measure for the length of the prong, measure the height of the stone (at each spot if the stone is irregular) and add 3/8″ to allow for the depth of the metal base and the allowance for the top turnover on the stone.

STEP 5: Set the square frame on the charcoal block and fit the prongs into the holes. Be sure that the flatted top lines up with the curve of the inner cut. Flux the surface and the prongs, and place two snippets of medium solder on the base

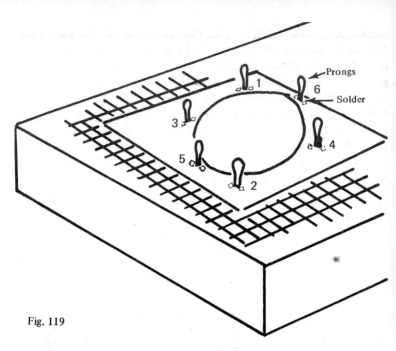

Fig. 119

touching each upright piece (see Fig. 119). Dry flux with soft flame, replacing bubbling solder bits with the poker. As the flux dries it will act like glue, holding all the parts in position. Use the tweezers to lift the piece and slip the wire mesh square on the charcoal block. Set the piece down on the wire mesh. Increase heat and play the flame around the outside of the base first, then into the hole in the center, to heat the entire bottom piece evenly before the uprights are heated. When the solder flashes, continue around the inner circle once or twice more to be sure that all the uprights are soldered in their holes. Turn off torch. Pickle, rinse and check soldering.

STEP 6: Use the flat needle file on back to level off any prong ends that protrude. Try not to scratch the silver as you work. Paint the base of each prong (front side) with ochre paste and set aside to dry.

STEP 7: Make the pendant loop or bale, by forming the 1¼" of scrap wire into an oval loop with the ends touching (not a continuous oval circlet). File the bottoms of the two ends flat to fit against the piece of tubing (see Fig. 120). Hold the loop with the tweezers while you flux it, dry with soft flame and melt two snippets of easy solder on the bottom. Set the tubing on the charcoal and flux. Reflux oval (still in tweezers). Hold the loop just above the tubing so that the tubing will heat from the edge of the flame you direct on the loop. When the solder starts to remelt set the loop on top of the tubing (at right angles to the way the tubing lies) and move the flame around it for another moment or two, just to be sure the solder grabbed. Then remove torch, and disengage tweezers. Pickle. Rinse. Set aside.

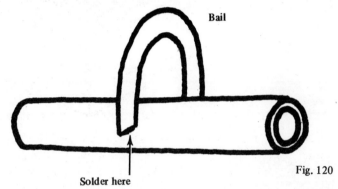

Bail

Solder here

Fig. 120

STEP 8: Turn silver frame upside down on charcoal block (prongs should balance it (see Fig. 121). Measure with pin tong to be sure your safety catch and joint ends are lined up exactly, and not too far apart. Use the scriber to mark the two spots with an X (see Fig. 122). Remember that the pin should balance properly when you wear it, and set the line of the pin tong above the center line of the frame. Remember, too, that the throat of the safety catch must face down for it to be useful, and that the little ears must be on top when it is soldered.

Fig. 121

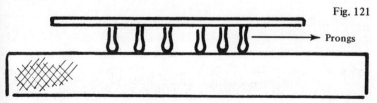

Prongs

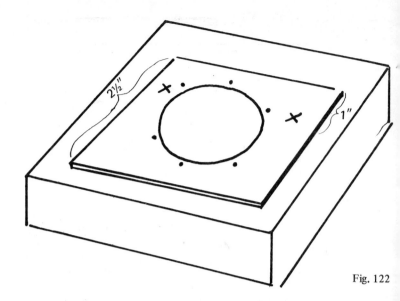

Fig. 122

STEP 9: Catch and joint ends are done one at a time, but method is the same. Hold piece in soldering tweezers; flux, dry, melt snippet of easy solder on base. Reflux. Flux base and dry. Set catch in place on X-mark. Put extra snip of easy solder on base touching catch. Heat base in wide circles around catch. Catch will get enough heat from this motion. Do not throw flame directly on the safety catch. Solder will run very soon. Remove heat at once. Repeat with joint end, lining up with your eye carefully, and being sure that the upright ends of the joint line up with the top and bottom of the frame rather than with the sides. When both parts are soldered, pickle, rinse and check the ears of the safety catch to be sure they move. They may be stiff at first.

STEP 10: Before assembling, polish. First rub with steel wool front, back and prongs too. You will find it easier, because of the prongs, to use small pieces of emery cloth and crocus cloth. Polish the bale too.

STEP 11: Assemble by putting stone in place and holding it down with one thumb while the prongs are pushed down into place with pliers. Do not work around the stone in order, as

176

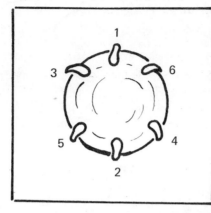

Fig. 123

you might push it out of position; do work across to help
anchor it (see Fig. 123). Press the prong in gently at the base
of the stone and down over the top of the stone at the tip of
the prong. Be careful not to scratch the stone or the silver.
Turn over and place the pin tong ears in the holes of the joint
catch. Close tightly with tips of flat-nosed pliers. Slide the
tubing in the pin tong before you close the safety catch (see
Fig. 124).

Bail

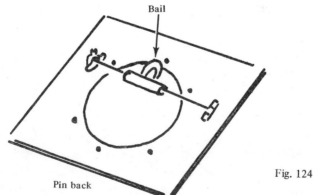

Pin back

Fig. 124

STEP 12: Rub front and back briskly with rouge cloth for a
high shine.

Design Interlude

The simplest setting for any stone or other object consists of just prongs. When you are designing a prong mounting think of the prongs as fingers, because that is the way they act. Fig. 125 shows prongs set up for a pendant that is made of three pieces of 18 gauge round wire, soldered together at a center point after the two outside wires have been bent into V-shapes. The center wire is longer, to allow for the top to be formed into a ring for the chain. The wire ends have been treated in the same manner as the Pin-Pendant. The same design (without the ring, if desired) can be made in 20 gauge wire for a tie-tack, or made up twice for earrings.

The prong setting is ideal for any object that is irregular in shape. When you want to mount an uncut stone specimen, a tumbled stone, a piece of coral, a shell, or a bit of polished wood, prongs are the answer. You can use as few as three prongs, or as many as ten, depending on the size of the piece and the number of spots where it needs to be anchored. You can use prongs alone, or attach them to a background, a frame, or even to a bezel.

Prongs are ideal, also, for setting stones with facets. This method of cutting and polishing gemstones is usually done for transparent gems, especially the fine, expensive

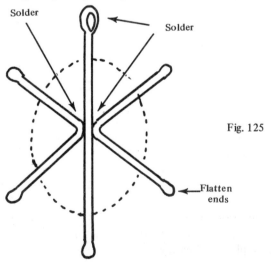

Solder

Solder

Fig. 125

Flatten ends

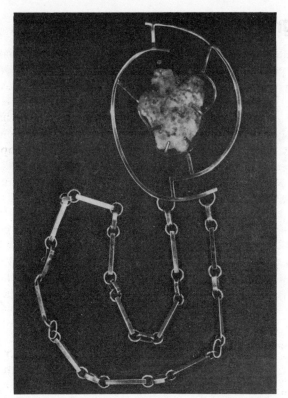

Plate 21: An uncut stone attached to an open background
of soldered square wires.

ones—diamonds, emeralds, topaz, ruby and many forms of
quartz. If such stones were mounted in bezels only the top
(table) would catch the light and the facetting would be
wasted. Prongs hold the stone above the surface of the
background and allow light to hit from all sides and to
bounce off the angles of the facets. This gives the stone great
brilliance and fire, and often increases, optically if not truly,
the size of the stone.

This does not mean that cabochon-cut stones cannot be
pronged with great effect. *You* must examine carefully each
object you wish to mount, and decide whether a frame will
give it needed importance, or if prongs alone will serve better
to display its beauty.

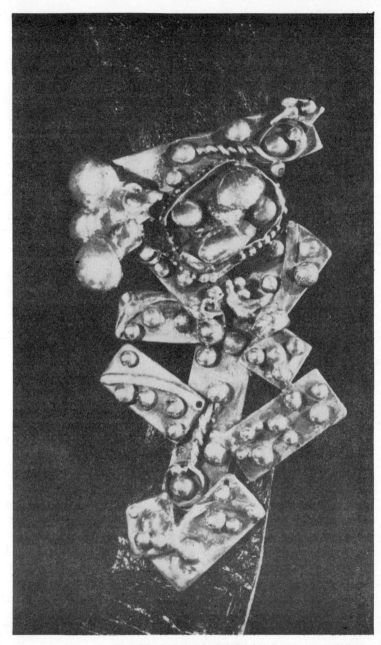

Plate 22: Fused silver belt buckle.

fusing

Fusing metal is one of the most interesting things you can do with your torch. Fusing means that the pieces of metal are permanently joined together without the use of solder, under the direct heat of the torch, which actually melts the surface of each metal and they join together in the cooling process. It is the ideal way to use up bits of scrap, since these bits laid out and examined from all angles, will suggest all sorts of design ideas. If you wish, you can make a paper pattern, and saw out pieces of silver to fit into the pattern for fusing. Then practice first on copper scraps, fusing them first to each other, and then to a base plate, all in one operation. It must be done carefully because too much heat will make the whole design collapse and melt into a blob. Then try laying the bits on the charcoal block and fusing them to each other without a base. The copper will take a little longer to fuse than silver will, but works much the same way. If you are making a ring or a buckle, the base is necessary. For earrings or a pendant, an open design may be prettier.

Belt Buckle

MATERIALS:

Scraps of silver: ends of twisted wire, left-over bits of
    flat plate, broken bezels, partly melted pieces—in short,
    all your disasters now become grist for your design mill
One 2" x 3" piece 16 gauge silver
Two 2½-inch pieces ¼ x 14 gauge rectangular wire
1¾-inch wide suede or leather strip, waist measure plus 5"

TOOLS:

Torch (#20)	Emery cloth (#30)
Flux and brush (#25 & 19)	Crocus cloth (#31)
Asbestos square (#21)	Polishing cloth (#33)
Wire mesh square (#22)	Liver of sulphate in
Charcoal block (#24)	solution (optional)
Soldering tweezers (#16)	Pumice powder and old
Poker (#14)	toothbrush
Easy solder (#29)	Hammer and two rivets
Pickling Solution (#27)	Flat-nosed pliers (#4)
Medium steel wool (#32)	Half-round file (#9)

Numbers refer to tools as identified and discussed in Chapter 3.

STEP 1: File rounded corners on the buckle blank and bevel edges all around the piece, working front and back with half-round file, flat side.

STEP 2: Check your pieces of scrap and decide which you will use. Lay them out on the buckle blank and move them around until you have found a pattern you like. Use them in a single layer, or build up in part of the pattern, laying pieces of scrap on top and across other pieces on the lower

Fig. 126

layer—make all the parts of your design touch each other, or leave bare spaces, too (see Fig. 126 for a suggestion). You might make a design in the center of the buckle and use other pieces of scrap to form a frame around the outer edges. If you are going to antique the finished piece you must leave some background bare to stay dark, so that the raised parts of the design will gleam brighter by contrast. If you make the entire design in the center, leave a clear border to frame the pattern around the edges.

STEP 3: Flux the entire piece. Dry with a soft flame. Be careful not to blow the parts out of position.

STEP 4: Increase the flame until you have a bright blue cone of light and play this over the entire piece. Heat the large (base) piece first by moving the flame around the edges, pointing it down through the wire mesh to the charcoal. Since the charcoal retains and reflects heat, it will heat the bottom of the blank while the torch flame is heating the top. Move the torch slowly over the piece. When the flux burns off you will see the silver bits glow red and then almost white as they form a molten skin. The base on which they rest should form a skin at the same time. Remove the heat when this happens. Turn off the torch. Put the piece in the pickling solution. Leave for a few minutes. Rinse in clear water and check to see that the piece is completely fused. You may have to reflux and reheat if you have any loose pieces. You will certainly have to repeat if you are building a second layer. This time do not concentrate on the base, just on the two layers of pieces, You may find that some of the thinner wires or smaller bits have balled up under the heat. Or you may have made balls of separate scrap pieces first, to use as part of your pattern.

STEP 5: With the flat-nosed pliers, turn down ½″ of the end of each bit of rectangular wire to make a small bridge of each piece. Fit each bridge on the back of the buckle across the 2″ measurement, one at each end, about ¾″ in from the side (see Fig. 127). File the bottoms of the bridges' ends flat to make a tight joint with the buckle back.

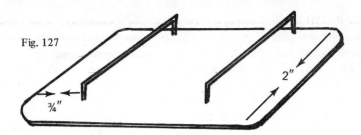

Fig. 127

¾"

2"

STEP 6: Flux the entire back of the buckle Set up the two bridges, with two snippets of easy solder touching each side of the bases (inside and out) on the buckle (see Fig. 128). You need eight bits of solder for each bridge. Dry with a soft flame, using the poker to push straying solder snips back into position. Increase the flame and solder both bridges with one operation. Remember to heat the base first, then the bridges, and last the seams.

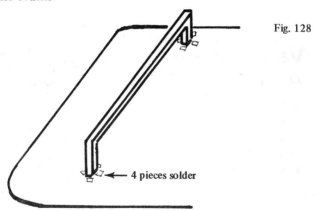

Fig. 128

← 4 pieces solder

STEP 7: Pickle (not while red-hot), rinse, dry and check soldering.

STEP 8: Rub entire back of buckle with No. 2/0 steel wool, then with crocus cloth to clean up completely. Turn over and rub edges of buckle and all spots where no metal pieces were fused. Use steel wool lightly over the fused design.

STEP 9: If you wish to antique it, lay piece in liver of sulphate solution for about 30 seconds. Rinse clean.

STEP 10: Use pumice powder or cleanser and old toothbrush and rub vigorously to remove excess dark color. Clean entire back, also.

STEP 11: Polish with steel wool pad, emery cloth and crocus cloth for a bright finish on all raised parts of the design. Buff with rouge cloth for final finish.

STEP 12: Assemble belt any one of the following ways. Ask your shoemaker to rivet one end of the leather to one of the bridges, and set grommets to fasten other end. Thread the leather through both bridges and fasten in back. (Tie if you use suede, use grommets if leather.) Use grommets to fasten leather to one bridge. Slide other end of the belt through both bridges to hold in place when you wear the belt.

Variations on the Theme: A Fused Pin-Pendant

MATERIALS:
Scraps of silver
Three-piece sterling pin back with safety catch
½-inch piece of tubing, 1/8″ in diameter
¾-inch piece 16 gauge half-round wire.

TOOLS:
Same as for Belt Buckle, plus Round-nosed plier (#3)

Number refers to tool as identified and discussed in Chapter 3.

STEP 1: The procedure for the pendant is the same as for the buckle, except that you are fusing the pieces of scrap to each other, not to a solid back. You must, therefore, be sure that all pieces touch at least two others, and if you build bits of scrap up across these joints you will have a stronger piece of jewelry (see Fig. 129).

Fig. 129

STEPS 2 and 3: Repeat Steps 2 and 3 of the Belt Buckle, but lay your bits of scrap out on the charcoal block. Where possible, overlap bits just a little.

STEP 4: With the round-nosed pliers, bend the ¾-inch piece of half-round wire so that the ends touch each other tightly. It is not necessary to form a continuous band. File the base of the two ends to fit against the ½-inch piece of tubing and use easy solder to solder together. Pickle, rinse and dry. Check soldering and set aside. This is the bale for your chain.

STEP 5: Use the scriber to mark on the back of the fused piece the spots where you will solder on the safety catch and the joint end of the pin back. Set them above the center line of the piece, so the pin will balance when it is worn. Measure the distance between them with the pin tong (the bar) so that they are not too far apart. Remember that they must line up *exactly* if the pin is to work well. The little ears of the safety catch must be on top of the catch, and the open throat should face down towards the bottom of the pin. You can slip a steel needle in to connect the two pieces so that they stay in line while you solder.

STEP 6: Flux the entire back and the bottoms of each cupped base on the catch and the joint end. Dry with a soft flame. Melt a snippet of easy solder into each little cup. Set each part on the mark, connect with the steel needle, and solder into place, being sure that you heat the base of first before you approach the findings with the torch. If you heat

186

Plate 23: Beads combine with fused-pattern links. Pendant is made of fused pieces soldered to silver.

the findings prematurely, you may fuse the ears so that the safety catch will not work. You should be able to see each little finding settle itself into place as the solder in the cup remelts. Remove the heat instantly. Turn off the torch, pickle, rinse and check soldering.

STEP 7: Set pin tong in place in the joint end (the little prongs will fit into the holes in the two sides) and close the sides with your pliers.

STEP 8: Repeat Step 11 of Belt Buckle to polish. When you wish to wear the piece as a pendant, slip the piece of tubing over the pin tong, fasten the safety catch, and thread a chain, ribbon or length of heavy embroidery silk through the bail on the tubing.

Ring

MATERIALS:
Pieces of scrap
Circle or oval of 18 gauge silver (¾" to 1" should
  be large enough)
One 2½-inch piece 14 gauge round wire

TOOLS:
Same as for Belt Buckle, plus
Ring mandrel (or dowel)
Mallet

STEPS 1 and 2: Repeat Steps 2 and 3 of Belt Buckle.

STEP 3: Anneal 14 gauge round wire. Form into ring shank (check for size) and file ends for tight joint. Solder together with 2 snips of hard solder. Pickle, rinse, dry and check soldering. File with half-round needle file to make seam line vanish. Ochre seam.

STEP 4: Set fused ring top face down on magnesium block. File smooth spot on ring shank opposite seam line. Flux both parts, after marking where shank will sit on the top. If the top is oval, you must decide first whether you wish the ring to lie across your finger or run the long way. Be sure, too, that when you make the mark for the seat of the ring shank that it runs across the line of the pattern on the front. Dry the top of the ring with a soft flame. Hold the ring shank in your soldering tweezers while you dry the flux on it. Set three or four snippets of easy solder along the mark where the shank is to sit and increase the flame. Melt the solder, holding the shank over the spot it is to sit on, and heating it a little at a time so that it is not as hot as the base until the last minute, as the solder *starts* to remelt, set the shank in place and hold it until the solder flashes. Remove heat instantly, but continue to hold the shank in place with the tweezers for another few moments. Drop into pickle (not the tweezers), rinse, dry and check soldering. (Rinse in hot water to remove ochre first.)

STEP 5: Paint on liver of sulphate solution with cleaned ochre brush if you wish to antique ring top. Wash it after 30 seconds and clean off excess with cleanser and old toothbrush, dampened.

STEP 6: Repeat Step 11 of Belt Buckle to polish. Don't forget the inside of the ring shank while you are polishing.

Design Interlude

It is difficult to suggest patterns for fusing because no two craftsmen have identical scrap collections. All bits of scrap are three-dimensional and the best fused designs are open in feeling instead of closed and dense. The shapes of the pieces will make their own suggestions. Lay them out on paper and turn them around. Several put together can suggest initials, or make a tree shape, or set up in an abstract pattern. Remember that the antiquing of the open spaces will emphasize the high spots and give depth to the design. Use the tendency that silver has to ball up under heat as part of your pattern. The effect you get when you apply heat may not be exactly the effect you got when you arranged the bits on paper, but what you do get will be interesting and have a texture you can get by no other means.

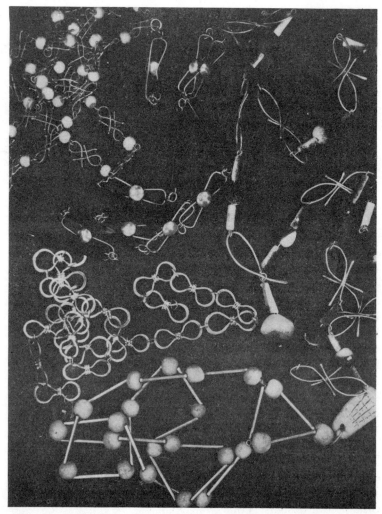

Plate 24: Chains to make and wear singly or in combination.

CHAPTER 17

chains

Chains can be made in almost any length and from almost any material or combination of materials. Soldered links are usual in well-made metal chains, but when metal is varied by combination with shells, beads of ceramic, ivory or stone, or other delicate objects, the links can be soldered only up to the point where the objects must be attached. The use of heat, after that, would ruin the stones.

The simplest chain is a sequence of linked rings. Sometimes round rings are linked in multiple arrangements. A link is pulled through two previous rings, or three, instead of one. Or a pair of rings is linked to another pair. This can be done with sets of three or four rings. Intricate patterning with rings is used to make ropes.

Links can be round, oval, square, oblong or free-form. They can be twisted by hand, or made on jigs; strung on connectors between the links or on the wire of the link itself. They can be made of strips of wire with soldered or fused ornamental designs. Your first chain will be made of circular links, flattened on two sides.

Round Wire Chain

MATERIALS:
One 8-foot piece 18 gauge round wire (this will make a
  30-inch chain)

TOOLS:

Hand-vise (#11)	Pickling solution (#27)
Dowel stick, ¾-inch diameter	Hammer and anvil (or metal
Saw frame & No. 1 blade	plate or old iron) (#6)
(#17 and #18)	Steel wool No. 4/0 (#31)
Torch (#20)	Fine emery cloth cut into
Asbestos square (#21)	2x3 inch oblongs (#30)
Charcoal block (#24)	Crocus cloth (#32)
Flux & brush (#25 and #19)	Rouge cloth (#33)
Ochre & brush (#28 & #19)	Half-round needle file (#10)
Hard and easy silver solder	Soldering tweezers (#16)
(#29)	

Number refer to tools as identified and discussed in Chapter 3.

STEP 1: Make a coil of the wire, tie with binding wire and
paint on a thin coat of flux. Anneal with soft flame. Quench
in pickle solution. Rinse, dry and straighten wire with fingers.

STEP 2: Set one end of the dowel stick in the hand vise.
Wrap the end of the wire tightly around the end of the dowel
stick, holding fingers of one hand on the wire and the dowel
stick as you turn the hand-vise with the other hand (see Fig.
130). The process is the same as for making jump rings—you

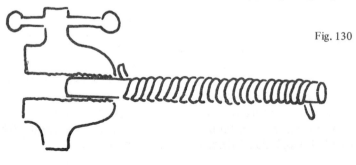

Fig. 130

192

are just making them larger this time. Keep the winding even and close together so that the rings will all be the same size. You should have 37 rings plus a small end of scrap wire. Slide off the dowel stick *after* you have threaded the saw frame, or the coil may loosen.

STEP 3: Saw the rings apart, being careful to saw on a straight line starting just where the last coil ends (see Fig. 131). Hold the coil together tightly to keep the rings uniform in size. If you saw carefully the ends will match and you will not have to file them for soldering.

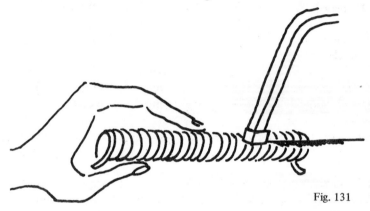

Fig. 131

STEP 4: Check the ends of each ring to see that they make a close fit. File with flat needle file, if necessary. Snap closed, using tension. Flux 18 rings, and solder, one at a time, with a snippet of hard solder for each. Keep the torch moving at all times, for wire burns easily. Pickle, rinse and dry. Check soldering.

STEP 5: Use the half-round needle file to file lightly across the seam line, inside and out, until it disappears. Set each ring in turn on an anvil, and hammer lightly with the flat face of the hammer to flatten two areas of the circlet that are opposite each other (see Fig. 132). Hammer front and back so you don't distort the ring. Be careful not to nick the wire with the edge of the hammer. Rub each ring front and back with steel wool. Paint rings with ochre, and dry.

193

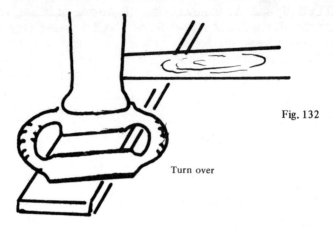

Fig. 132

Turn over

STEP 6: Connect each pair of rings with a third ring. Close for tight fit and flux center ring only (see Fig. 133). Repeat soldering, using medium solder this time. Rinse ochre off with hot water before you pickle, rinse and dry.

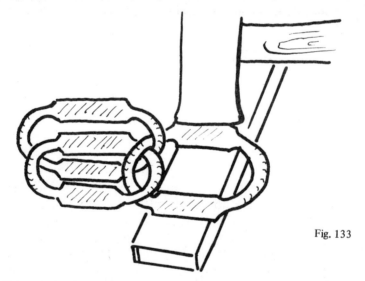

Fig. 133

STEP 7: Repeat Step 5 with newly soldered rings, filing off seam lines before you flatten the two opposite areas. Be careful to lay *only* the section of the ring to be flattened on the anvil. Keep your blows even. If you hammer where two wires cross you may break the wire.

STEPS 8 and 9: Connect the triple-ring sections with 9 additional rings, and repeat Steps 4 and 5, using easy solder snippets. Check the length before you solder the last rings closed. It should slip easily over your head and require no closing device. You can remove or add links to suit yourself.

STEP 10: Polish by using the pieces of emery and crocus cloth folded in half, over each ring in turn, so you clean both sides at one time. Use the rouge cloth for a high shine.

Variations on the Theme: Beaded Chain

MATERIALS:
One 8-foot piece 18 gauge round wire
20 beads approximately 10mm. in size (beads may be glass or
   stone in any shape you choose)

TOOLS:

The same as for Round Wire Chain	Both pairs of pliers (#4 and #5)
One-inch mandrel	Minus hammer and anvil

Numbers refer to tools as identified and discussed in Chapter 3.

Steps 1-4: This chain requires two different links. The first is made as for the Round Wire Chain by wrapping on a one-inch mandrel, but they are not flattened. Instead, pull them into an oval shape and then twist figure-8s. The second link is the connector, a straight piece of wire strung with a bead, with ringed ends left unsoldered. Repeat Step 1 of Round Wire Chain. Cut 20 pieces of wire, each 1½″ long. Set aside. With remaining wire, repeat Steps 2, 3 and 4 of Round Wire Chain, making 20 rings. File away seam line.

STEP 5: Use the round-nosed pliers and your fingers to pull each ring into a long narrow oval. Keep the seamed part up

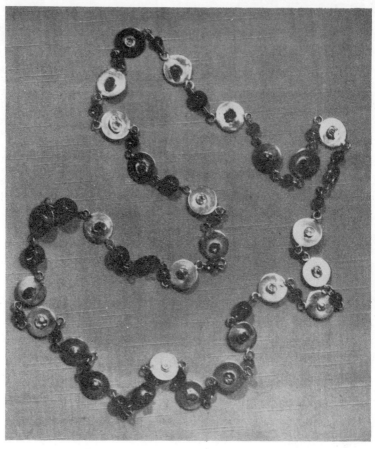

Plate 25: Chain with tiny cups soldered to round disc with
glass beads used for accent.

near the top (see Fig. 134). True the rounded ends on the
largest part of the pliers. Polish with the emery and crocus
cloth pieces. Hold the top loop with the round-nosed pliers

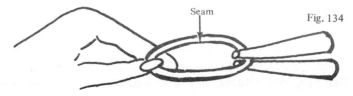

Seam

Fig. 134

Fig. 135

(either across the wires or hanging on the largest part of the nose, whichever is more comfortable for you) and with the other hand set the flat-nosed pliers across the bottom loop. Twist twice to the right to make a figure-8 with a double-crossed center (see Fig. 135). Be careful not to scratch the wires. Set aside.

STEP 6: Make a ring on one end of each small piece of wire, thread on the bead and make partly open ring on other end. Use the round-nosed pliers and make rings large enough so that the bead uses almost all of the center section of each piece. Close these rings to connect figure-8s into a chain. (Check for length before you attach the last four links—you may find that you have enough links to make a chain plus earrings. The figure-8s make attractive earrings hanging by themselves, or can be combined with the beaded connectors.)

Motif Chain

MATERIALS:
One 3-foot piece 16 gauge round wire
One 6-foot piece 20 gauge round wire

TOOLS:

Same as for Round Wire Chain No. 5 knitting needle
  plus Jig Pair of No. 4 needles for
Substitute Wire cutter dowel stick

STEP 1: First make the jig. You may draw the pattern directly on the wood, if you like. Drive the nails inside the design line. Remember that the purpose of the nails is to

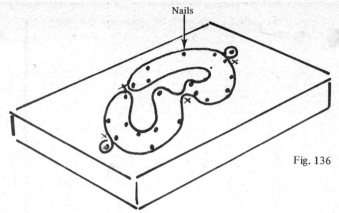

Fig. 136

make the wire hold a shape, so put the nails closer together around a curve (see Fig. 136). Cut the nail heads off with the wire cutter so the pattern will slide off.

STEP 2: Anneal the 16 gauge wire and make eight motifs—each one using just over 4″ of the wire. If you have made very complicated designs, you may need more wire to work them out. In order for the motifs to be permanent designs, you will have to solder wherever the wires cross or touch. Mark solder points with Xs (see Fig. 136). If you flux the entire shape and lay snippets of hard solder across both wires you can solder the whole thing at one time. Pickle, rinse, dry, check soldering and set aside.

STEPS 3-5: Anneal the 20 gauge wire and after straightening, cut into two lengths: one 56″ long, the other 16″ long. Wrap the longer piece on the No. 5 knitting needle to make 56 round rings. Repeat Steps 4, 5 and 6 of the Round Wire Chain, but solder closed (with hard solder) only 18 rings. Make up 18 sets with 3 rings each and set aside (see Fig. 137).

Saw here

Fig. 137

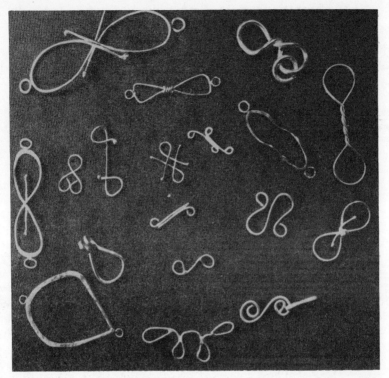

Plate 26: Links can be any size or shape.

STEPS 6-8: Connect the pair of No. 4 Knitting Needles with scotch tape and use as a mandrel to wrap the 16-inch length of wire, making nine oblong links (see Fig. 138). File the ends of each, if necessary, for tight joint and solder closed with hard solder. Repeat Steps 4 and 5 of Round Wire Chain. Then connect oblong links to open round links (two for

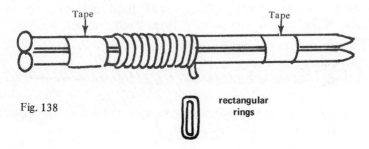

Tape   Tape

Fig. 138   rectangular
rings

199

each). Repeat Step 6 of Round Wire Chain (no hammering)—using medium solder—to make nine small lengths of chain, each containing a centered oblong link and 2 sets of triple rings, with end rings still open.

STEP 9: Connect the motifs with the open rings (see Fig. 139). Repeat soldering steps with easy solder.

STEP 10: Clean and polish with pieces of fine emery cloth and crocus cloth. Shine with the rouge cloth.

Fig. 139

Design Interlude

Links can be of any size or shape. The larger the link, the fewer you need to make. The long chains should fit over your head comfortably and need no closing. For most of them, you can allow seven links (this is not a measure for large links) to make 2″ of chain. Check your own links for an accurate measure. Keep a notation of link size and measure so you can duplicate chains at will.

You must be careful not to make links too large. Sometimes a design, handsome in a smaller version, does not translate well, and looks awkward because it does not hang well on the body. Consider too, the background that will fill the empty spaces of the links. A single space link can be filled with color and design in fabric, but a more complicated link needs a solid background to bring out the richness of its design.

You can figure required wire by multiplying the diameter of the link by 3½, then deciding on the number of links you will need for the length of chain you want, and multiplying by that figure. Always make a few extra links. Even if you end up with some of them in your scrap box, you can always use them to make earrings.

There's a wide choice of wire. Choose carefully, for upon your choice depends the success of the project (and the ease of construction). For instance, you could use 8 gauge wire to make the Round Wire Chain and the individual links would look well, but the weight of the finished chain might be uncomfortable.

Remember this: the smaller the link, the finer the wire. Heavy wire is out of proportion as well as more difficult to coil; round wire is the easiest to coil evenly and the easiest to file for a tight joint in soldering; flat wire is easiest to use for flat links. It is easiest to use for soldered-on decorations, and holes bored at both ends make for simple construction with jump-ring connectors; beads are accents only—in a chain, make the silver the important part of the design.

The jig you make should not be too complicated. Remember that where the wires cross each other or touch, they must be soldered, or they will not hold the shape with constant wearing. And the more soldering you must do, the more chance of accidents.

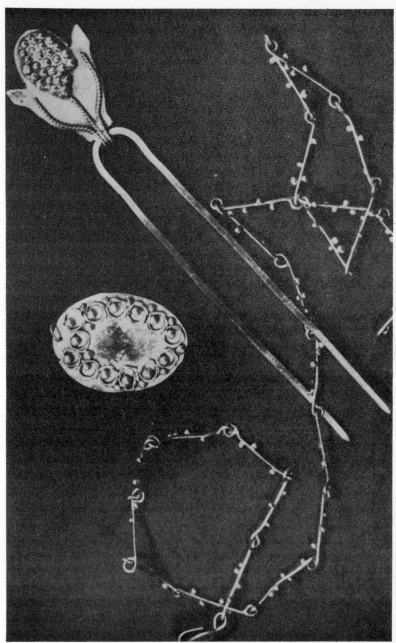

Plate 27: Jewelry decorated with granulation and filigree.

202

granulation & filigree

Jewelry decorated with granulation and filigree work has been popular since ancient times in areas as far apart on the globe as Mexico, India and the Middle East. Granules are very small shot (round balls) in traditional work, but modern craftsmen-jewelers very often use small square or oblong pellets to create beautiful designs. The granules are fused to the background in a decorative pattern, using a chemical formula instead of soldering, but the tiny balls might melt under the heat of the torch. You are going to do simulated granulation, making larger shot and using solder to attach them. The same patterned blank can be turned into a pendant, if you prefer.

Hairpin

MATERIALS:
One 1" x 1¼" piece 20 gauge silver
One 10-inch piece 16 gauge round wire
One 16-inch piece 20 gauge round wire
One 8-inch piece 24 gauge round wire (optional)

TOOLS:

Saw frame and No. 1 blade
 (#17 and #18)
Flat file (#8)
Half-round needle file
 (#10)
Hammer and nail (#6)
Hand drill and cup hook
 (#13)
Bench vise (#12)
Poker (#14)
Plate shear (#5)
Round-nosed plier (#3)
Tweezers (#15)
Torch (#20)

Asbestos square (#21)
Charcoal block (#24)
Pickling solution (#27)
Flux and brush (#25 & #19)
Ochre and brush (#28 & #19)
Hard and easy silver solder
 (#29)
Medium emery cloth (#30)
Crocus cloth (#32)
Rouge cloth (#33)
Paper, soft pencil, rubber
 cement
No. 2 Knitting needle
Hand vise

Numbers refer to tools as identified and discussed in Chapter 3.

STEP 1: Anneal the 20 gauge round wire and wrap on the No. 2 knitting needle, making a close tight coil. You will need 25 balls, but you might make a few extra; they are always useful. Cut them apart with the plate shear and lay four rings on the charcoal block, one near each corner, but not right at the edge. Flux. Light the torch and play the flame (blue cone) on the ring in a circular motion until the silver begins to contract. Once it balls up move to the next one and do all four rings before you use the tweezers to drop them in the pickle solution. You will have a little flat spot on the bottom of each ball, but since they are to be soldered to a flat surface, this does not matter. To make perfectly round balls—and there will be times when you need to—make a

204

small dent in the charcoal block where each ring lies, so the formed ball will slide into the dent and be round bottomed (see Fig. 140). When you have made all your balls, rinse and dry them and set aside.

Fig. 140

Charcoal block dented
for round balls

STEP 2: Outline the blank on paper. Draw a center line through the long dimension and draw half of your pattern. Keep it simple and allow for one area where you can mass the granules. Fold on the line and transfer the design by rubbing the back of the paper. Go over all lines to make them sharp. Glue paper to silver blank with rubber cement. Dry thoroughly.

STEP 3: Anneal the 24 gauge wire (carefully—it is very fragile). Fold in half and set loose ends tightly into the bench vise. Tighten cup hook into hand drill chuck and slide wire loop over hook. Twist to make a tight rope. Loosen ends from hook and bench vise (see Fig. 102). Shape to conform to pattern lines, using fingers and round-nosed pliers. Cut to size and set aside.

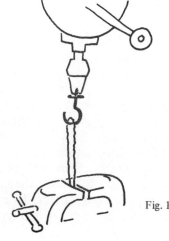

Fig. 102

205

STEP 4: Thread the saw frame with No. 1 blade and cut out the shape of your background. Save your scraps. Use the half-round needle file to round all corners and bevel all edges.

STEP 5: Test with some of your granules to see how closely together they fit on the design area, then remove them and use the hammer and nail to make a very shallow dent in each spot where a granule should sit. Use the scriber to scratch through the paper the lines where the small lengths of filligree wire will go (see Fig. 141). Soak off the paper and dry. Go over lines for definition, if necessary. Set aside.

Fig. 141

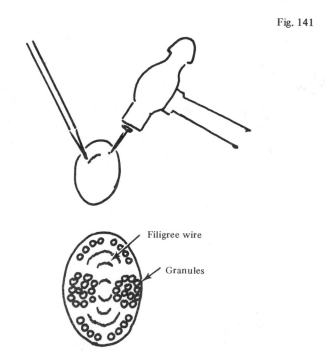

Filigree wire

Granules

STEP 6: Anneal the piece of 26 gauge round wire, and bend in half to make a narrow U-shape. File a small spot on the top of the U and on the base of your patterned blank until they will make a tight joint and bind them together with iron binding wire. Flux both parts and dry with a soft flame. Set snippets of hard solder in place with tip of the flux brush, two on each side of the bottom of the blank, lying on the U. Increase flame and solder the two together. Remove binding wire and place in pickle solution. Rinse, dry, check soldering.

STEP 7: Use needle file, front and back, to file across seam line until it disappears. Then paint entire seam with ochre paste. Set the wire mesh screen on the charcoal block and set hairpin on that (see Fig. 142). Allow to dry.

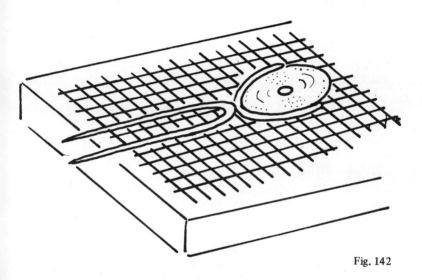

Fig. 142

STEP 8: Hold the flat file with one end resting on a piece of clean paper and rub easy solder strip on the file to make a small pile of filings. You cannot cut solder in pieces as small as you will need. Spread these filings around and between the granules which you have set in place in the little dents on the design. Don't be stingy; you can always make more filings if you need them, and you can store leftovers in a tiny medicine bottle. (Mark it, so you don't forget that these are solder not silver filings.) Scatter a little of the solder dust along side of each of the twisted wire strips.

STEP 9: Flux entire area gently. *Don't* displace the parts of your pattern and try not to remove the solder. Dry with a very soft flame, then increase heat and keep flame moving over the entire piece. Do not get the point of the flame too close to the wire or the granules. Heat the base first, by directing the heat down around the edges of the piece through the wire mesh to the charcoal beneath, so that the heat will be reflected to the back of the piece too. When the flux burns over and the base glows, you should see the solder flash. Circle the flame once or twice directly over the granulated area to be sure that all the solder grabbed. Remove heat.

STEP 10: Rinse, *in a dish,* to remove ochre, just in case any of the balls are still loose. Resolder with more filings if necessary. Pickle, rinse and dry. If you have to resolder, ochre the joint *and* areas that *are* soldered.

STEP 11: Use the flat file first, then the half-round needle file, to taper the bottom inch of each prong and round the ends. Make sure the ends are smooth.

STEP 12: Go over entire piece with No. 2 steel wool, then with the medium emery and the crocus cloth. Use the rouge cloth for a high shine. *NOTE:* If you like, use the liver of sulphate to antique the silver near the filigree wires and the granulated area. If you do this, use an old toothbrush and cleanser to clean off excess blackening before polishing.

Variations on the Theme: Pendant

MATERIALS:
Same as for Hairpin, except substitute a ¾" or 1" scrap of
  silver for the 16 gauge round wire to make a necklace bale
Constructed or commercial chain

STEPS 1-5: Repeat Steps 1-5 of Hairpin.

STEP 6: Fold the bit of scrap (a not-too-heavy bit of half-round wire is ideal) in half so that ends lie flat against each other (not a continuous circlet). File the ends smooth to meet top of the designed blank in a tight joint, and solder with hard solder. If you prefer, you can drill a hole in the top of the blank and insert a jump ring (solder it closed) in place of the bale (see Fig. 143).

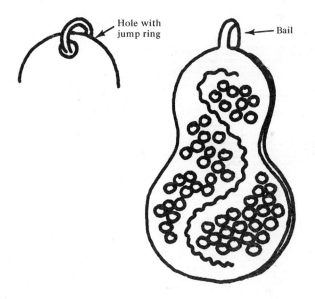

Hole with jump ring

Bail

Fig. 143

Ring

MATERIALS:
One 18 gauge ring blank in desired ring size

TOOLS:
Same as for Hairpin, plus
Magnesium block

STEP 1: Use dowel stick and mallet to curve ring ends (see Fig. 144). Use needle file to smooth and bevel all edges. File ends straight across to make a tight joint. Close with tension or bind with wire, and solder closed, using two or three snippets of hard solder. Remove binding wire (if you used it) before you pickle. Rinse, dry, and check soldering. File across seam with needle file (flat side on outer seam, round side on inner seam) to make seam line vanish. Paint seam with ochre paste. Set aside to dry.

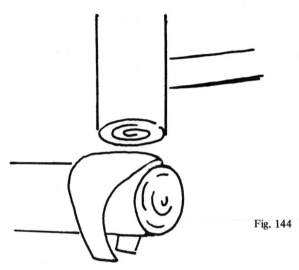

Fig. 144

STEPS 2 and 3: Repeat Steps 1 and 3 of Hairpin.

STEPS 4-8: Repeat Steps 2, 5, 8, 9 and 10 of Hairpin. To solder on the granules for Step 9, balance the ring between the charcoal block and the magnesium block, with the formed shank hanging down between them.

STEP 9: Repeat Step 12 of Hairpin.

Design Interlude

Designs made with filigree and granulation are always airy and delicate in feeling. Often the filigree wires are used to form a pattern within a frame of heavier wire, with no background at all—soldering for this is very painstaking.

Design granulation can be realistic or free-form, single layered or built-up, but the areas to be filled with balls should be kept small. If you try to make too elaborate a pattern, you may find that you have problems in attaching all the balls and wires at one time. Each time you must use solder, you risk endangering the unit.

The size of the granules can be varied by using larger silver rings, and large balls can be added to designs using other techniques, to make beautiful finishing touches. They make good accents for the spots where bezels join ring shanks. You might try filigree wires and/or the granules to accent a pierced design, or to form a ring around a bezel for a stone, or to solder on or next to wire strips for a necklace.

Plate 28: Spoke pendant frames an agate.

accidental shapes

You can have two kinds of accidents when making jewelry. One of these is done on purpose to give you an accidental shape. Although this kind of shape can never be duplicated, it can, with effort, be approximated.

The other kind is the real accident—the "Oh what did I do!" After one of these you put down your tools, take a deep breath, and think of suicide. A second look will help you decide whether salvage is possible. Sometimes salvage is easy. The agate pendant, center piece in Plate 28, was started as the center of a wire bracelet. In the soldering, such care was taken *not* to burn the bezel that one of the square wire spokes was melted. Cutting away a matching portion of the outer wire frame, and the substitution of a hanger and jump ring, turned a catastrophe into an attractive pendant.

The free-form pendant, top piece in the same photograph, was semi-accidental. The frame was made from 10 gauge round wire, used with 8 gauge half-round to twist into a bangle. When the half-round wire and the round wire were disengaged (the bracelet was open curved half-round only) the curves of the round wire were loosened and made irregular as it was detached. These loose curves suggested the shape of the pendant, so the two ends were set side by side,

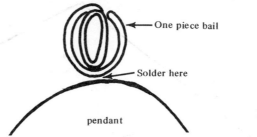

One piece bail

Solder here

pendant

Fig. 145

filing flat on top to join the one-piece bale (see Fig. 145), and bound into position for soldering with hard solder. The shape was then forged to flatten, and the bezel (open-backed) was soldered in place across two of the wire curves.

There are several ways to make accidental shapes to use. It is difficult to estimate the materials because the amount of scrap you must use depends on what is in your scrap box. If the scraps are heavy gauge you will use less. Experiment for yourself. Make a pile of scrap pieces on the charcoal block, heat with a strong flame until the pile melts and forms a blob. Make several piles of different sizes and see how much scrap you need to make different size blobs. To make the dropped shapes of accidental form, you will need blobs about 5/8" in size. If you have made several blobs they can be remelted, one at a time.

Set the charcoal block at one end of the asbestos square, to expose as much of the square as possible on the side away from you. Melt the blob or a small pile of scrap and use the flame of the torch to push it off the charcoal block so that it drops on the asbestos square (see Fig. 146). As it drops it will broaden and thin out and form a shape. Make several shapes and decide if they are interesting enough to be usable. Remelt the ones you don't like and try again. The shapes will be too thin to stand up to wear by themselves, but you can solder several to form a pattern for a belt buckle, or use a single one as part of a ring.

The pendant with the hanging stone, Plate 28 bottom piece, was made by soldering two accidental shapes to a backing of square wire. One piece of round wire was threaded through the holes of a piece of rough coral, then twisted to form a loop for a chain.

214

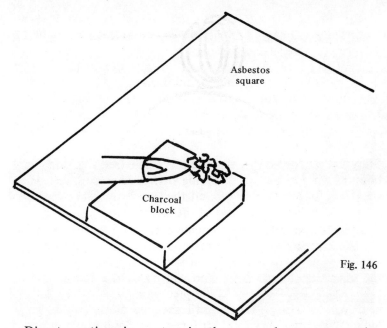

Asbestos
square

Charcoal
block

Fig. 146

Direct casting in water is the second way to make interesting accidental shapes, solid and cupped. Although no two shapes will be identical, you *can* make very similar shapes by measuring the amount of scrap silver you use each time, using the same amount of water each time, and by dropping the melted silver from the same height each time. You can use a purchased crucible (it comes in two pieces with a handle) and flux the inside heavily before you use it. Or you can make a crucible (one-piece) by hollowing out a small bowl in a charcoal block, and making a channel from the hollow to the edge for pouring (see Fig. 147). You will

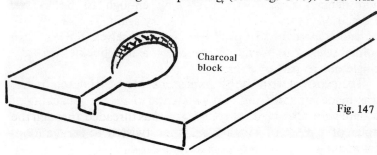

Charcoal
block

Fig. 147

need long-handled tongs for handling this safely. It will eventually crack and break down from the heat, but not before you have made considerable use of it.

You will find that experimenting with this form of casting is as much fun as making granulations. Melt your measured pile of scrap in your crucible (without flux in the purchased

Plate 29: A welcome accident.

one—you already melted a good layer of flux on the inside; with flux, if you are using charcoal). You need quite high heat to melt this scrap down. When it is molten, it is poured into a bowl or pan of cold water. If you pour from only a small distance (say, a few inches) you will get a solid blob of silver. If you increase the height you will get spread-out shapes and irregular cups. You will soon learn to control the height of the pouring and the depth of the water to get the kind of shape you want.

Two other accidental treatments can be done with a torch. You can make holes in the metal as part of your design. The shapes and sizes of these holes will almost always be accidental, since the size and shape of a burned hole is hard to control. You can also distress the surface with reticulation.

For this form of surface texturing, the metal is heated with the torch until it forms a skin, just as in fusing. When the skin begins to ripple the heat is removed, and the metal is cleaned and examined to see if the desired degree of texture has been achieved. It is wise to use the heavier gauges (at least 16 gauge) of silver for this, because it is a tricky process requiring that the torch be removed at exactly the right moment so the metal is not burnt through. Use pieces of your scrap to experiment with this technique until you learn just where to stop this new game this side of destruction.

By this time you will have developed what we call a "seeing eye." When you try to duplicate a design, you are using your eyes for the most exacting kind of seeing—seeing *through* the obvious pattern to the technique of construction. The repetition of that technique, once perceived, requires coordination of eye, brain and hand.

The design need not be man-made. Nature is by far the best of designers. You have examined natural objects for their basic shapes and translated some of those shapes to your own designs. You have looked at work in other craft fields and used those shapes for translation. You have learned to use your eyes for *seeing* rather than casual *looking* and you have harnessed your imagination to your eyes, so that everything and anything will be grist to your mill.

One of your bonus by-products in all this is the development of appreciation. You can recognize good technique in your own craft, and in other crafts. You have learned that the most polished technician is not necessarily the finest designer—but the finest design is degraded by shoddy workmanship! The creative imagination, harnessed to a seeing eye and a pair of capable hands is a winning combination every time.

Good luck! And enjoy your work with silver.

Reference Lists

GEM STONES

COLOR & TYPE*	NAME	HARDNESS**	USUAL CUT	COMMENTS
RED (T)	Ruby	9	Facet	"Star" stone—cab. cut. Try synthetics.
Deep red (TL)	Garnet	7½	Facet/cab.	A lovely stone—the green is unusual.
Rose-red (O)	Rhodonite	Med. hard	Cab, Tumble	Look for "spiderwebs."
Pink-red (O)	Rhodochrosite	Brittle	Cab	Bands of color—needs careful work.
Pink (T)	Rose Quartz	7	Facet/tumble	Pretty, often milky.
Red-Brown (TL)	Carnelian	7	Facet, Cab, Tumble	Lovely color variations.
GREEN	Emerald	8	Facet	Try synthetics.
Yellow-green (TL)	Peridot	7	Facet	
Silvery (TL)	Amazonite	6	Cab	Very pretty in silver.
Apple (TL)	Chrysprase	7½	Cab	Lovely color.
Blue-green (TL)	Chrysocolla	7½	Cab	Looks like malachite. Easier to work with.
Dark green	Malachite	4½	Cab	Often banded color darkens with wear.
Dark green to White (O to TL)	Jade and Jadeite	6	Cab or carved	Value increases with translucence.
Green or pink & green (TL)	Tourmaline	7½	Facet, cab, rough	Great variety of color—watermelon is beautiful.

**Hardness Numbers are the Mohs Scale with 10 hardest.
Stones with hardness of 6 and over are safest to work with.

*O = Opaque

T = Transparent

TL = Translucent

COLOR & TYPE*	HARDNESS** NAME	USUAL CUT	COMMENTS
Green (day) Violet (night) (TL)	Alexandrite 8	Facet	
YELLOW (T)			
Yellow (T)	Topaz 8	Facet	Often sold as topaz and just as lovely.
	Citrine 7	Facet	"Stars" are cab. Try synthetics.
BLUE (T)	Sapphire 9	Facet	Often gold-flecked.
Deep blue (O)	Lapis Lazuli 7	Cab, carve	White-flecked, the "poor-man's lapis."
Deep blue (O)	Sodalite 6	Cab	Best has no green (Persian).
Blue to blue-green (O)	Turquoise Soft, porous	Cab	Deep color best.
Light blue blue-green (T)	Aquamarine 7½	Facet	A new discovery from South Africa, brilliant, very beautiful and expensive.
Clear, medium-deep blue (TL)	Tanzanite 7½	Facet	Often found with malachite. Gorgeous but soft, take care.
Brilliant (TL)	Azurite 3½ to 4	Cab	Often sold as "smokey topaz" —lovely. "Cairgorm"
BROWN			
Golden to smokey (T)	Smokey Quartz 7½	Facet	Justly popular.
Golden streaks (TL)	Cat's Eye 8	Cab, tumble	A lovely stone for silver.
VIOLET (T to TL)	Amethyst 7	Facet	Soft tones—good to work with.
Grey-lavender (TL)	Chalcedony 7	Cab	

*O = Opaque

T = Transparent

TL = Translucent

**Hardness Numbers are the Mohs Scale with 10 hardest.

Stones with hardness of 6 and over are safest to work with.

GEM STONES CONTINUED

COLOR & TYPE*	NAME	HARDNESS**	USUAL CUT	COMMENTS
BLACK — GREY				
With metallic lustre (0)	Hematite	6	Cab, carve	"Black diamond"
Silvery—often iridescent (0)	Obsidian	5½	Cab, tumble	Many varieties—some handsome.
MIXED COLORS				
Clear, green marking (T)	Moss Agate	7	Cab, tumble	Gorgeous.
Flashes of light (TL)	Opals	5	Cab, facet	Absolutely gorgeous, but hard to work with. "Black" is best.
Mixed colors and patterns (0)	Jaspers Banded and Lace Agates	7	Cab	Interesting markings and colors. Easy to work with.
CLEAR (T)	Diamond	10—Hardest	Facet	
Clear (T)	Crystal	7½	Facet	

*0 = Opaque

T = Transparent

TL = Translucent

**Hardness Numbers are the Mohs Scale with 10 hardest. Stones with hardness of 6 and over are safest to work with.

GEM STONES THAT ARE NOT STONES

COLOR & TYPE*	NAME	SOURCES	USUAL CUT	COMMENTS
Milky sheen (many shades)	Pearls	Oyster	Beads	Fresh water pearls and baroques are very interesting.
Honey-red brown (T to TL)	Amber	Fossil, resin	Cab, facet	But so lovely.
Cream to brown (0)	Ivory	Tusks (bone)	Cab, carve	Much fake ivory on market—watch out.
White-pink-red (0)	Coral	Ocean, fossil	Cab, carve, beads	Oxblood and "angel-skin" most expensive.
Black (0)	Coral	Hawaii	Cab, beads	
Shiny black (0)	Jet	Fossil, coal	Facet	"The funeral jewel." Not popular now.
Various (0 to TL)	Cameos	Stone or shell	Carved	A fine antique cameo is a real work of art.

**Hardness Numbers are the Mohs Scale with 10 hardest. Stones with hardness of 6 and over are safest to work with.

*0 = Opaque

T = Transparent

TL = Translucent

metal gauges

American metal refiners and suppliers use the Brown & Sharp Scale of gauge measurements, but it is well to know standard measurements of those gauges, in order to decide which gauge is necessary. Many suppliers sell silver by weight as well as gauge, so the B&S Scale is translated for you by thickness in inches and millimeters and weights per square inch, for the gauges you are most likely to want.

TABLE OF GAUGES

B&S SCALE	INCHES	MILLIMETERS	WEIGHT
4	.204	5.189	1.120
6	.162	4.111	.884
8	.128	3.264	.701
10	.101	2.588	.556
12	.080	2.052	.441
14	.064	1.651	.350
16	.050	1.270	.277
18	.040	1.016	.220
20	.032	.813	.174
22	.025	.635	.138
24	.020	.508	.110
26	.015	.381	.086
28	.012	.305	.069

SHEET

B & S Gauge		ROUND B & S Gauge
12		9 ●
14		12 ●
16		16 •
18		18 •
20		20 ·
22		24 ·
24		
26		

WIRE

HALF ROUND B & S Gauge	SQUARE B & S Gauge	RECTANGULAR B & S Gauges
5/16" base	8	4 x 16
6	12	6 x 18
10	14	8 x 22
15	18	

225

solders

Hard silver solders can be purchased in sheet or wire form, or precut. It is most economical to cut your own snippets from sheet solder. Following is a chart of solder steps and the temperature at which each flows.

SOLDER TABLE & CHART

NAME	FLOWS AT
Hard	$1435°$ F
Medium	$1390°$ F
Easy	$1325°$ F
Extra-Easy	$1305°$ F

Note that sterling silver melts at $1640°$ F.

craft organizations

Almost every state now has regional or local craft organizations, since interest in the crafts has intensified during the past few years. Many local memberships, both professional and amateur, are in all the crafts; some local chapters specialize in one craft alone. It would be worth your while to investigate the programs offered by your local group, as a source of information, for the exchange of ideas, and for a chance to see the work of other jewelry craftsmen. Membership is usually nominal. To find the group nearest you, write to:

American Crafts Council
44 West 53rd Street
New York, N.Y. 10019

Canadian Guild of Crafts
140 Cumberland Street
Toronto, 5, Ontario

or

2025 Peel Street
Montreal, Quebec
c/o Ruthadel Anderson
1170 Saimanu Street
Honolulu, Hawaii 96814

sources & suppliers

AKG & Company
1114 Greentree Road
Newark, Del. 19711
Tools, metals, findings.

Allcraft Tool & Supply
  Company, Inc.
100 Frank Road
Hicksville, N. Y. 11801 and
22 West 48 Street
New York, N. Y. 10036
*Tools, metals, equipment,
  stones, findings.*

Anchor Tool & Supply Co.,
  Inc.
12 John Street
New York, N. Y. 10038
*Tools, findings, metals,
  equipment.*

ÁRE Creations
Box 155 E, No. Montpelier
  Road
Plainfield, Vt. 05667
Tools, supplies, metals.

Bartlett & Co., Inc.
5 South Wabash Ave.
Room 819
Chicago, Ill. 60603
Tools, supplies, metals.

The Bead Game
505 North Fairfax Ave.
Los Angeles, Calif. 90036
*Beads, metals, stones,
  findings.*

Bergen Arts & Crafts
14 Prospect Street (Box 381)
Marblehead, Mass.
Tools, findings, metals.

Boin Arts & Crafts Co.
87 Morris Street
Morristown, N. J. 07960
Tools, metals.

California Crafts Supply
1096 No. Main Street
Orange, Calif. 92667
Tools, equipment, metals.

Grieger's Inc.
1633 East Walnut Street
Pasadena, Calif. 91109
Findings, metals.

T. B. Hagstoz & Son
709 Sansom Street
Philadelphia, Pa. 19106
*Tools, metals, stones,
   findings, supplies.*

C. R. Hill Co.
2734 West 11 Mile Road
Berkley, Michigan 48072
Tools, equipment, findings.

Francis Hoover
12445 Chandler Blvd.
No. Hollywood, Calif. 91607
Stones.

Metal City Findings Corp.
450 West 31 Street
New York, N. Y. 10001
Findings.

NASCO
Fort Atkinson, Wisc. 53538
*Tools, metals, findings,
   equipment.*

New Orleans Jewelers
      Supply Co.
206 Charter Street
New Orleans, La. 70130
Tools, equipment, supplies.

Nordman & Aurich
657 Mission Street
San Francisco, Calif. 94080
Tools, supplies, findings.

David Rose
26-10 Glenwood Road
Brooklyn, N. Y. 11210
Stones.

Rosenthal Jewelers
   Supply Corp.
117 N.E. 1st Avenue
Miami, Florida 33132
Tools, equipment.

Sax Crafts
207 N. Milwaukee Street
Milwaukee, Wis. 53202
Tools, supplies.

C. W. Somers & Co.
387 Washington Street
Boston, Mass. 02108
Tools, metals, findings.

Southwest, Inc.
1712 Jackson St.,
P.O. Box 2010
Dallas, Texas 75221
    and
118 Broadway, Box 1298
San Antonio, Texas 78295
Metals, tools, findings.
    and
1725 Victory Blvd.
Glendale, Calif. 91201
*Tools, equipment, findings,
    metals.*

Technical Specialties
    International Inc.
487 Elliott Avenue West
Seattle, Wash. 98119
Tools, equipment, supplies.

Tepping Studio Supply Co.
3003 Salem Avenue
Dayton, Ohio 45406
*Tools, equipment, findings,
    metals.*

Thetacraft, Inc.
P. O. Box 483, Dept TWC
Valley Cottage, N. Y. 10989
Unusual beads.

Norman A. Thomas Co., Inc.
742 North Woodward Avenue
Birmingham, Mich. 48011
Tools, equipment, supplies.

Myron Toback, Inc.
23 West 47th Street
New York, N. Y. 10036
Findings, metals.

glossary

ALLOY: A metal hybrid composed of two or more metals combined when the parent metal lacks desired qualities (hardness, color, etc.).

ANNEALING: A process of heating metal and then quenching it in cold water, in order to make the metal workable. This is the method used for all nonferrous (iron) metals.

ANVIL: Any piece of hardened steel, either shaped or in block form, on which metal is hammered in the forging process.

ASBESTOS BOARD: A non-burning mineral, pressed into sheets of varying thickness. Used as a fire-retarding base for soldering equipment.

BALE: A cap-shaped or ring-shaped form used for pendant stones or metal shapes, through which the neck-chain is passed.

BLANK: The piece of metal sheet from which a designed piece is to be formed.

BEVEL EDGE: An angled edge. When a piece of silver is beveled from the front and from the back, a rounded edge is formed for a finished look.

BEZEL: A metal frame; the part of a setting that holds the jewel safely and permanently in position.

BUFF: The wooden stick covered with leather or polishing cloth. Also comes in wheel form for machine use with grinding and polishing compounds.

BURR: Rough point left on edge of metal by coarse filing or cutting.

CABOCHON: A domed cut, usually on semi-precious stones of either round or oval shape. Usually flat-backed, but some stones are domed front and back. Often referred to as "cabs." Height of stone depends on marking and color.

CARAT: Unit of weight for precious and semi-precious stones.

CHASING: A method of decorating the surface of the metal by hammering on shaped punches.

CHUCK: The portion of a tool (usually a drill) that holds the working part in position, by screwing tight when the replaceable part is inserted.

CROCUS CLOTH: A polishing cloth impregnated with a metallic oxide.

CRUCIBLE: A pot of heat-resistant substance (like porcelain) used for melting metal for casting.

DIRECT CASTING: The process of dropping molten silver directly into cold water to form shapes.

DRILL BIT: Small part used with hand or machine drill for boring holes in metal. Comes in 80 sizes.

EMERY CLOTH: A polishing cloth impregnated with granular corumdum. Coarser than Crocus cloth and always used first.

232

FACET: One of a series of small places (faces) cut into a hard (transparent) gem-stone.

FILIGREE: A technique of ornamental metal design using fine wires to form patterns, without or with background. Popular in Near East, India, Mexico.

FINDINGS: The small pieces, often mechanical, used to connect or attach jewelry pieces. Also available are coin mounts, barrettes, tie-clasps, tie tacks and finials.

FINE SILVER: "Pure" silver, composed of 999 parts of silver out of 1000. It is too soft for jewelry, but it is used for enamelling and for bezel wire.

FLUX: A borax compound used to retard oxidation and to help induce solder to flow.

FORGING: The process of shaping metal by hammering over an anvil. During the forging process annealing is necessary to prevent work-hardening of the metal.

FUSING: Attaching metal pieces to each other by direct heat which melts the surfaces where the pieces touch.

GAUGE: A measure of thickness. On the Brown & Sharp Scale used in the United States, the lower the gauge number, the heavier the metal.

GRANULATION: A decorative technique using metal balls of various small sizes either as accents or to fill pattern areas. Often used with filigree wires.

HARD ROLLED (HARD DRAWN): Metal fabricated this way MUST be annealed before working. Where "spring" is necessary, hard drawn metal is used. If you have a choice get silver that has already been annealed.

INNER BEZEL: A ring of wire soldered to the inside of the bezel frame to form a shelf on which the jewel sits.

JIG: A template or design pattern, made to guide the material into the shape of the pattern. The simplest jigs are made of nails in wooden blocks.

LIVER OF SULPHATE: A potassium sulphide solution mixed with water and used to antique silver. Store in closed jar and discard when skum forms on top.

MANDREL: Any solid rod of metal or wood, used as a core to shape a piece of jewelry, such as a ring or bracelet mandrel.

NITRIC ACID: A colorless, corrosive chemical used for etching metal and for cleaning oxidation (in mild solution). Commercial substitutes that are safer are recommended for home use.

OCHRE: A yellow compound of earth, iron-bearing, used with oil as a painting color. Mixed with water it acts to deter solder flow and protects already-soldered joints.

OXIDATION: "Fire scale" darkened spots on silver due to too much heat on unprotected surfaces. Scale is reduced by the use of flux. It can be removed by pickling and intensive polishing.

PICKLING SOLUTION: A chemical and water solution used to clean metal, especially after soldering.

PIERCING: The creation of a design in metal by the use of drilled holes and the jeweler's saw.

PIN JOINT: The separate finding soldered to the back of the piece into which the rivet end of the pin tong is locked.

PIN TONG: The needle-like part of the pin that passes through the material. One end is permanently fastened into the pin joint.

PUNCHES: Metal pieces with patterned faces, used with hammers to texture or pattern a metal blank. Punches are usually made of hardened steel.

RETICULATION: The formation by the use of direct heat of web-like or veined patterns on the face of the metal. An interesting decorative technique requiring great care.

ROUGE: A ferris oxide paste used to give a final polish to metal pieces.

SHANK: The portion of a ring that encircles the finger.

SHOT: Small silver balls (see granulation) used as decoration in jewelry.

SOLDER: Metal alloys that flow at a lower degree of heat than the basic metal to be joined. Comes in wide variety for hard silver soldering.

SPECIMEN STONES: Semi-precious stones in their natural state—uncut and unpolished. Many forms of rough specimens are inexpensive and useable for jewelry. Check to find out if stones are too brittle or too soft for mounting.

STAMPING: A method of surface texturing. See punches.

STERLING SILVER: An alloy of 925 parts silver, 75 parts copper (for hardness). The name comes from its use as the standard for English coinage. American coins were 900 silver; South American silver can be anything from 800 up; European (old) silver is usually better than 900.

TABLE CUT: The flat top of a facetted stone (usually square or rectangular in shape). Round facetted stones usually have only a small centered flat area.

TUMBLED STONES: Stones that have been smoothed and polished either by natural forces (waves and ocean sand) or in a machine using chemical grits. They are almost always free-form and are best used in cages, wrapped in silver wires, or attached with prongs.

WORK HARDENED: The condition of silver that has been bent or hammered. The metal must be annealed frequently during these processes to keep it workable. Work-hardened silver is subject to stress and may crack.

bibliography

SUGGESTED READING FOR FURTHER STUDY

Boulay, R. *Make Your Own Elegant Jewelry,* Sterling Publishing Co., New York, 1972

Bovin, Murray. *Jewelry Making For Schools, Tradesmen and Craftsmen,* Published by the author, New York, N.Y. 1964.

Choate, Sharr. *Creative Gold and Silversmithing,* Crown Publishers, New York, 1970

Clegg, Helen & Mary Larom. *Jewelry Making for Fun & Profit,* David McKay Co., New York, 1951

Crawford, John. *Introducing Jewelry Making,* Watson-Guptil Publications, New York, 1969

Davidson, Ian. *Ideas for Jewelry,* Watson-Guptill Publications, New York, 1972

Franke, Louis E. *Handwrought Jewelry,* McKnight & McKnight Publishing Company, Bloomington, Ill., 1962

Gentile, Thomas. *Step by Step Jewelry,* Golden Press, New York, 1963 (paper)

Ginnett, Elsie. *Make Your Own Rings & Other Things,* Sterling Publishing Co., New York, 1973

Glass, F. J. *Jewelry Craft,* University of London Press, England, 1928. Reprinted Newton K. Gress, Calif., 1971 (paper)

Hemord, Larry. *Creative Jewelry Making,* Doubleday & Co., New York, 1975 (paper)

Hornung, Clarence. *Source Book of Antiques & Jewelry Designs,* George Braziller, New York, 1968

Martin, C. J. & V. D'Amico. *How to Make Modern Jewelry,* Museum of Modern Art, New York, 1949

Maryon, Herbert. *Metalwork & Enamelling,* 5th Revised Edition, Dover Publications, New York, 1971 (paper)

Morton, Philip. *Contemporary Jewelry,* Holt, Rinehart & Winston, New York, 1976 (paper)

von Newman, Robert. *Design & Creation of Jewelry,* Chilton Book Co., Radnor, Pa., 1972

Pack, Greta. *Jewelry & Enameling,* D. Van Nostrand Co., Princeton, N. J. 1941

Rose, A. F. & A. Cirino. *Jewelry Making & Design,* 4th Revised Edition, Dover Publications, New York, 1967 (paper)

Untracht, Oppi. *Metal Techniques for Craftsmen,* Doubleday & Co., Garden City, N. Y. 1968 (paper)

Wood, Louise & Orvelo. *Make Your Own Jewelry,* Grosset & Dunlop, New York, 1975 (paper)